ABOUT THE EDITOR

SIMON VAN BOOY is the author of *The Secret Lives of People in Love* and *Love Begins in Winter*, which in 2009 won the Frank O'Connor International Short Story Award. He has written for *The New York Times*, *The Daily Telegraph*, *The Times*, *The Guardian*, and NPR. He lives in New York City where he lectures at the School of Visual Arts and is involved in the Rutgers Early College Humanities program for young adults living in under-served communities. His work has been translated into nine different languages.

WHY WE NEED LOVE

ALSO BY SIMON VAN BOOY

FICTION

Love Begins in Winter

The Secret Lives of People in Love

NONFICTION

Why We Fight (editor)

Why Our Decisions Don't Matter (editor)

WHY WE NEED LOVE

Edited by Simon Van Booy

HARPER**PERENNIAL** **x** MODERN**THOUGHT**

NEW YORK • LONDON • TORONTO • SYDNEY • NEW DELHI • AUCKLAND

HARPER**PERENNIAL** ⬤ MODERN**THOUGHT**

HarperCollins books may be purchased for educational, business, or sales promotional use. For information, please write: Special Markets Department, HarperCollins Publishers, 10 East 53rd Street, New York, NY 10022.

FIRST EDITION

Designed by Justin Dodd

Library of Congress Cataloging-in-Publication data is available upon request.

ISBN 978-0-06-184554-3

10 11 12 13 14 OV/RRD 10 9 8 7 6 5 4 3 2 1

*This book is dedicated to my mother and father,
Joan and Stephen, for whom love is a
journey with no destination*

CONTENTS

PREFACE TO THE SERIES

My hope for these books is to present interesting and exciting philosophical ideas in a straightforward, but intelligent, language that can be understood by everyone. I believe that philosophy is a subject we have a natural gift for, but a subject often regarded as one with no practical value—and closed to anyone outside the walls of universities. I am committed to the idea that these central questions of life are part of our everyday lives—that we all possess the skill and agility to tackle them, and that by pondering them, we can experience more fulfillment in our relationships, in our work, and in how we view ourselves.

Inside these books are readings, poems, quotations, and visual images that will inspire you to continue exploring the subject for years to come. I have tried my best to present philosophical ideas with no immediate resolution as immediately accessible for everyday thinking.

These volumes are not meant to convince you of anything, to be a definitive source, or to offer any new insights on a topic. Their purpose is simply to introduce you to an age-old theme that quite possibly has already taken a key role in your life.

To begin then, let me tell you about a small statue I once saw in a New Orleans public park. The young man of marble who stood before me (discolored by years of affection from birds) was holding a book to his heart with one hand, while using his other hand to pick a grape from a vine.

If the grape were to represent life, and the book over his heart, knowledge, then one interpretation may be that book learning and actual life experience complement each other. So by reading about other people's experiences in this book, we may begin to understand ourselves with fresh insight. Reading reassures us that no matter how alone we might feel, there are many others—spread as wide as history itself— who have felt the same way we have, who have occupied the rooms we find ourselves locked in at various points of our lives.

One celebrated aspect of literature is that unlike the ambitious exactitude of science, literature is often ambiguous—meaning that two people might have very different ideas about what a play, poem, or book is about. While at first this implied vagueness might seem detrimental to literature, it's one of its sustaining virtues, and allows people from different cultures, and even different time periods, to learn something about their own lives from a single story. If a story were viewed as a literal history, one could argue that it wouldn't be quite as useful—because history is traditionally viewed as a record of what we think happened, whereas story and myth are more like advice whispered to us by a wise grandmother. Many of the great geniuses who lived over the last five thousand years were not writers at all, but oral storytellers who left it up to others to write down what they said.

Stories, parables, and dialogues were their preferred method of teaching—in other words, instead of saying to a lazy child: "Go tidy your room now!" our greatest thinkers would probably have begun with something like: "There was once a girl who never tidied her room . . ."

INTRODUCTION

As you read this introduction, someone, somewhere, is falling in love; a child is calling out to someone in the darkness as he awakes from a bad dream; someone is sitting alone in a car missing someone as rain pelts the windshield; someone is leaning on a desk, anticipating happiness he hopes love will one day bring him; and perhaps someone very old is looking out a window, wishing he had said yes instead of walking away on that snowy afternoon in 1951.

No matter what we do, love saturates our lives in every possible way. Even when we try to escape, it finds us—if merely to tease us with what we could have had.

Through the readings, paintings, quotes, ideas, and confessions within these pages, we are going to explore why we seem so desperately to need love, but also why we need to give it.

WHY WE NEED LOVE

The hunger for love is much more difficult to remove than the hunger for bread.

—*Mother Teresa*

George Eliot (whose real name was Mary Ann Evans) was born in 1819 in rural England. As a young woman, she lost her religious faith (her father blamed it on her "intellectual friends"), and when her father died in her thirtieth year, she moved to London and became a writer. In London, she developed an intimate friendship with George Henry Lewes, whom she was unable to marry because Lewes was already married (though estranged from his wife). Evans and Lewes shocked their friends and family in 1854 by deciding to openly live together. It was at this point in her life, cut off from so many people, that Evans started writing fiction. Not wishing to draw attention to her unconventional life, the name "George Eliot" was chosen as a pseudonym. She died in 1880.

Silas Marner is about the life of a lonely weaver who finds an unlikely visitor inside his cottage one evening. The sight of the visitor fills Marner with a sudden and desperate feeling of love—a feeling that gives meaning to his life and frees him from a state of emotional isolation imposed on him by temperament and circumstance.

Eliot considered *Silas Marner* to be her masterpiece.

George Eliot

from *Silas Marner*

In the days when the spinning-wheels hummed busily in the farmhouses—and even great ladies, clothed in silk and thread-lace, had their toy spinning-wheels of polished oak— there might be seen in districts far away among the lanes, or deep in the bosom of the hills, certain pallid undersized men, who, by the side of the brawny country-folk, looked like the remnants of a disinherited race. The shepherd's dog barked fiercely when one of these alien-looking men appeared on the upland, dark against the early winter sunset; for what dog likes a figure bent under a heavy bag?—and these pale men rarely stirred abroad without that mysterious burden. The shepherd himself, though he had good reason to believe that the bag held nothing but flaxen thread, or else the long rolls of strong linen spun from that thread, was not quite sure that this trade of weaving, indispensable though it was, could be carried on entirely without the help of the Evil One. In that far-off time superstition clung easily round every person or thing that was at all unwonted, or even intermittent and occasional merely, like the visits of the pedlar or the knife-grinder. No one knew where wandering men had their homes or their origin; and how was a man to be explained unless you at least knew somebody who knew his father and mother? To the peasants of old times, the world outside their own direct experience was a region of vagueness and mystery: to their untravelled thought a state of wandering was a conception as dim as the winter life of the swallows that came back with the spring; and even a settler, if he came from distant parts, hardly ever ceased to be viewed with a remnant of distrust, which would have prevented any surprise if a long course of inoffensive conduct on his part had ended in the commission of a crime; especially if he had any reputation for knowledge, or showed any skill in handicraft. All cleverness, whether in the rapid use of that difficult instrument the tongue, or in some other art unfamiliar to villagers, was in itself suspicious: honest folk, born and bred in a visible manner, were mostly not overwise or clever—at least, not beyond such a matter as knowing the signs of the weather; and the process by which rapidity and dexterity of any kind were acquired was so wholly hidden, that they partook of the nature of conjuring. In this way it came to pass that those scattered linen-weavers—emigrants from the town into the country—were to the last regarded as aliens by their rustic neighbours, and usually contracted the eccentric habits which belong to a state of loneliness.

In the early years of this century, such a linen-weaver, named Silas Marner, worked at his vocation in a stone cottage that stood among the nutty hedgerows near the village of Raveloe, and not far from the edge of a deserted stone-pit. The questionable sound of Silas's loom, so unlike the natural cheerful trotting of the winnowing-machine, or the simpler rhythm of the flail, had a half-fearful fascination for the Raveloe boys, who would often leave off their nutting or birds'-nesting to peep in at the window of the stone cottage, counterbalancing a certain awe at the mysterious action of the loom, by a pleasant sense of scornful superiority, drawn from the mockery of its alternating noises, along with the bent, tread-mill attitude of the weaver. But sometimes it happened that Marner, pausing to adjust an irregularity in his thread, became aware of the small scoundrels, and, though chary of his time, he liked their intrusion so ill that he would descend from his loom, and, opening the door, would fix on them a gaze that was always enough to make them take to their legs in terror. For how was it possible to believe that those large brown protuberant eyes in Silas Marner's pale face really saw nothing very distinctly that was not close to them, and not rather that their dreadful stare could dart cramp, or rickets, or a wry mouth at any boy who happened to be in the rear? They had, perhaps, heard their fathers and mothers hint that Silas Marner could cure folk's rheumatism if he had a mind, and add, still more darkly, that if you could only speak the devil fair enough, he might save you the cost of the doctor. Such strange lingering echoes of the old demon-worship might perhaps even now be caught by the diligent listener among the grey-haired peas-

SIMON VAN BOOY

antry; for the rude mind with difficulty associates the ideas of power and benignity. A shadowy conception of power that by much persuasion can be induced to refrain from inflicting harm, is the shape most easily taken by the sense of the Invisible in the minds of men who have always been pressed close by primitive wants, and to whom a life of hard toil has never been illuminated by any enthusiastic religious faith. To them pain and mishap present a far wider range of possibilities than gladness and enjoyment: their imagination is almost barren of the images that feed desire and hope, but is all overgrown by recollections that are a perpetual pasture to fear. "Is there anything you can fancy that you would like to eat?" I once said to an old laboring man, who was in his last illness, and who had refused all the food his wife had offered him. "No," he answered, "I've never been used to nothing but common victual, and I can't eat that." Experience had bred no fancies in him that could raise the phantasm of appetite.

And Raveloe was a village where many of the old echoes lingered, undrowned by new voices. Not that it was one of those barren parishes lying on the outskirts of civilisation—inhabited by meagre sheep and thinly-scattered shepherds: on the contrary, it lay in the rich central plain of what we are pleased to call Merry England, and held farms which, speaking from a spiritual point of view, paid highly-desirable tithes. But it was nestled in a snug well-wooded hollow, quite an hour's journey on horseback from any turnpike, where it was never reached by the vibrations of the coach-horn, or of public opinion. It was an important-looking village, with a fine old church and large churchyard in the heart of it, and two or three large brick-and-stone homesteads, with well-walled orchards and ornamental weathercocks, standing close upon the road, and lifting more imposing fronts than the rectory, which peeped from among the trees on the other side of the churchyard: a village which showed at once the summits of its social life, and told the practised eye that there was no great park and manor-house in the vicinity, but that there were several chiefs in Raveloe who could farm badly quite at their ease, drawing enough money from their bad farming, in those war times, to live in a rollicking fashion, and keep a jolly Christmas, Whitsun, and Easter tide.

It was fifteen years since Silas Marner had first come to Raveloe; he was then simply a pallid young man, with prominent short-sighted brown eyes, whose appearance would have had nothing strange for people of average culture and experience, but for the villagers near whom he had come to settle it had mysterious peculiarities which corresponded with the exceptional nature of his occupation, and his advent from an unknown region called "North'ard." So had his way of life: he invited no comer to step across his door-sill, and he never strolled into the village to drink a pint at the Rainbow, or to gossip at the wheelwright's: he sought no man or woman, save for the purposes of his calling, or in order to supply himself with necessaries; and it was soon clear to the Raveloe lasses that he would never urge one of them to accept him against her will—quite as if he had heard them declare that they would never marry a dead man come to life again. This view of Marner's personality was not without another ground than his pale face and unexampled eyes; for Jem Rodney, the mole-catcher, averred that one evening as he was returning homeward he saw Silas Marner leaning against a stile with a heavy bag on his back, instead of resting the bag on the stile as a man in his senses would have done; and that, on coming up to him, he saw that Marner's eyes were set like a dead man's, and he spoke to him, and shook him, and his limbs were stiff, and his hands clutched the bag as if they'd been made of iron; but just as he had made up his mind that the weaver was dead, he came all right again, like, as you might say, in the winking of an eye, and said "Good night," and walked off. All this Jem swore he had seen, more by token that it was the very day he had been mole-catching on Squire Cass's land, down by the old saw-pit. Some said Marner must have been in a "fit," a word which seemed to explain things otherwise incredible; but the argumentative Mr. Macey, clerk of the parish, shook his head, and asked if anybody was ever known to go off in a fit and not fall down. A fit was a stroke, wasn't it? And it was in the nature of a stroke to partly take away the use of a man's limbs and throw him on the parish, if he'd got no children to look to. No, no; it was no stroke that would let a man stand on his legs, like a horse between the shafts, and then walk off as soon as you can say "Gee!" But there might be such a thing as a man's soul being loose from his body, and going out and in, like a bird out of its nest and back; and that was how folks got over-wise, for they went to school in this shell-less state to those who could teach them more than their neighbours could learn with their five senses and the parson. And where did Master Marner get his knowledge of herbs from—and charms too, if he liked to give them away? Jem Rodney's story was no more than what might have been expected by anybody who had seen how Marner had cured Sally Oates, and made her sleep like a baby, when her heart had been beating enough to burst her body, for two months and more, while she had been under the doctor's care. He might cure more folks if he would; but he was worth speaking fair, if it was only to keep him from doing you a mischief.

It was partly to this vague fear that Marner was indebted for protecting him from the persecution that his singulari-ties might have drawn upon him, but still more to the fact that, the old linen-weaver in the neighbouring parish of Tarley being dead, his handicraft made him a highly welcome set-tler to the richer housewives of the district, and even to the

SIMON VAN BOOY

more provident cottagers, who had their little stock of yarn at the year's end. Their sense of his usefulness would have counteracted any repugnance or suspicion which was not confirmed by a deficiency in the quality or the tale of the cloth he wove for them. And the years had rolled on without producing any change in the impressions of the neighbours concerning Marner, except the change from novelty to habit. At the end of fifteen years the Raveloe men said just the same things about Silas Marner as at the beginning: they did not say them quite so often, but they believed them much more strongly when they did say them. There was only one important addition which the years had brought: it was, that Master Marner had laid by a fine sight of money somewhere, and that he could buy up "bigger men" than himself.

But while opinion concerning him had remained nearly stationary, and his daily habits had presented scarcely any visible change, Marner's inward life had been a history and a metamorphosis, as that of every fervid nature must be when it has fled, or been condemned to solitude. His life, before he came to Raveloe, had been filled with the movement, the mental activity, and the close fellowship, which, in that day as in this, marked the life of an artisan early incorporated in a narrow religious sect, where the poorest layman has the chance of distinguishing himself by gifts of speech, and has, at the very least, the weight of a silent voter in the government of his community. Marner was highly thought of in that little hidden world, known to itself as the church assembling in Lantern Yard; he was believed to be a young man of exemplary life and ardent faith; and a peculiar interest had been centred in him ever since he had fallen, at a prayer-meeting, into a mysterious rigidity and suspension of consciousness, which, lasting for an hour or more, had been mistaken for death. To have sought a medical explanation for this phenomenon would have been held by Silas himself, as well as by his minister and fellow-members, a wilful self-exclusion from the spiritual significance that might lie therein. Silas was evidently a brother selected for a peculiar discipline; and though the effort to interpret this discipline was discouraged by the absence, on his part, of any spiritual vision during his outward trance, yet it was believed by himself and others that its effect was seen in an accession of light and fervour. A less truthful man than he might have been tempted into the subsequent creation of a vision in the form of resurgent memory; a less sane man might have believed in such a creation; but Silas was both sane and honest, though, as with many honest and fervent men, culture had not defined any channels for his sense of mystery, and so it spread itself over the proper pathway of inquiry and knowledge. He had inherited from his mother some acquaintance with medicinal herbs and their preparation—a little store of wisdom which she had imparted to him as a solemn bequest—but of late years he had had doubts about the lawfulness of applying this knowledge, believing that herbs could have no efficacy without prayer, and that prayer might suffice without herbs; so that his inherited delight to wander through the fields in search of foxglove and dandelion and coltsfoot, began to wear to him the character of a temptation.

Among the members of his church there was one young man, a little older than himself, with whom he had long lived in such close friendship that it was the custom of their Lantern Yard brethren to call them David and Jonathan. The real name of the friend was William Dane, and he, too, was regarded as a shining instance of youthful piety, though somewhat given to over-severity towards weaker brethren, and to be so dazzled by his own light as to hold himself wiser than his teachers. But whatever blemishes others might discern in William, to his friend's mind he was faultless; for Marner had one of those impressible self-doubting natures which, at an inexperienced age, admire imperativeness and lean on contradiction. The expression of trusting simplicity in Marner's face, heightened by that absence of special observation, that defenceless, deer-like gaze which belongs to large prominent eyes, was strongly contrasted by the self-complacent suppression of inward triumph that lurked in the narrow slanting eyes and compressed lips of William Dane. One of the most frequent topics of conversation between the two friends was

Assurance of salvation: Silas confessed that he could never arrive at anything higher than hope mingled with fear, and listened with longing wonder when William declared that he had possessed unshaken assurance ever since, in the period of his conversion, he had dreamed that he saw the words "calling and election sure" standing by themselves on a white page in the open Bible. Such colloquies have occupied many a pair of pale-faced weavers, whose unnurtured souls have been like young winged things, fluttering forsaken in the twilight.

It had seemed to the unsuspecting Silas that the friendship had suffered no chill even from his formation of another attachment of a closer kind. For some months he had been engaged to a young servant-woman, waiting only for a little increase to their mutual savings in order to [announce] their marriage; and it was a great delight to him that Sarah did not object to William's occasional presence in their Sunday interviews. It was at this point in their history that Silas's cataleptic fit occurred during the prayer-meeting; and amidst the various queries and expressions of interest addressed to him by his fellow-members, William's suggestion alone jarred with the general sympathy towards a brother thus singled out for special dealings. He observed that, to him, this trance looked more like a visitation of Satan than a proof of divine favour, and exhorted his friend to see that he hid no accursed thing

SIMON VAN BOOY

within his soul. Silas, feeling bound to accept rebuke and admonition as a brotherly office, felt no resentment, but only pain, at his friend's doubts concerning him; and to this was soon added some anxiety at the perception that Sarah's manner towards him began to exhibit a strange fluctuation between an effort at an increased manifestation of regard and involuntary signs of shrinking and dislike. He asked her if she wished to break off their engagement; but she denied this: their engagement was known to the church, and had been recognized in the prayer-meetings; it could not be broken off without strict investigation, and Sarah could render no reason that would be sanctioned by the feeling of the community. At this time the senior deacon was taken dangerously ill, and, being a childless widower, he was tended night and day by some of the younger brethren or sisters. Silas frequently took his turn in the night-watching with William, the one relieving the other at two in the morning. The old man, contrary to expectation, seemed to be on the way to recovery, when one night Silas, sitting up by his bedside, observed that his usual audible breathing had ceased. The candle was burning low, and he had to lift it to see the patient's face distinctly. Examination convinced him that the deacon was dead—had been dead some time, for the limbs were rigid. Silas asked himself if he had been asleep, and looked at the clock: it was already four in the morning. How was it that William had not come? In much anxiety he went to seek for help, and soon there were several friends assembled in the house, the minister among them, while Silas went away to his work, wishing he could have met William to know the reason of his nonappearance. But at six o'clock, as he was thinking of going to seek his friend, William came, and with him the minister. They came to summon him to Lantern Yard, to meet the church members there; and to his inquiry concerning the cause of the summons the only reply was, "You will hear." Nothing further was said until Silas was seated in the vestry, in front of the minister, with the eyes of those who to him represented God's people fixed solemnly upon him. Then the minister, taking out a pocket-knife, showed it to Silas, and asked him if he knew where he had left that knife? Silas said, he did not know that he had left it anywhere out of his own pocket—but he was trembling at this strange interrogation. He was then exhorted not to hide his sin, but to confess and repent. The knife had been found in the bureau by the departed deacon's bedside—found in the place where the little bag of church money had lain, which the minister himself had seen the day before. Some hand had removed that bag; and whose hand could it be, if not that of the man to whom the knife belonged? For some time Silas was mute with astonishment: then he said, "God will clear me: I know nothing about the knife being there, or the money being gone. Search me and my dwelling; you will find nothing

SIMON VAN BOOY

but three pound five of my own savings, which William Dane knows I have had these six months." At this William groaned, but the minister said, "The proof is heavy against you, brother Marner. The money was taken in the night last past, and no man was with our departed brother but you, for William Dane declares to us that he was hindered by sudden sickness from going to take his place as usual, and you yourself said that he had not come; and, moreover, you neglected the dead body."

"I must have slept," said Silas. Then after a pause, he added, "Or I must have had another visitation like that which you have all seen me under, so that the thief must have come and gone while I was not in the body, but out of the body. But, I say again, search me and my dwelling, for I have been nowhere else."

The search was made, and it ended—in William Dane's finding the well-known bag, empty, tucked behind the chest of drawers in Silas's chamber! On this William exhorted his friend to confess, and not to hide his sin any longer. Silas turned a look of keen reproach on him, and said, "William, for nine years that we have gone in and out together, have you ever known me tell a lie? But God will clear me."

"Brother," said William, "how do I know what you may have done in the secret chambers of your heart, to give Satan an advantage over you?"

Silas was still looking at his friend. Suddenly a deep flush came over his face, and he was about to speak impetuously, when he seemed checked again by some inward shock, that sent the flush back and made him tremble. But at last he spoke feebly, looking at William.

"I remember now—the knife wasn't in my pocket."

William said, "I know nothing of what you mean." The other persons present, however, began to inquire where Silas meant to say that the knife was, but he would give no further explanation: he only said, "I am sore stricken; I can say nothing. God will clear me."

On their return to the vestry there was further deliberation. Any resort to legal measures for ascertaining the culprit was contrary to the principles of the church in Lantern Yard, according to which prosecution was forbidden to Christians, even had the case held less scandal to the community. But the members were bound to take other measures for finding out the truth, and they resolved on praying and drawing lots. This resolution can be a ground of surprise only to those who are unacquainted with that obscure religious life which has gone on in the alleys of our towns. Silas knelt with his brethren, relying on his own innocence being certified by immediate divine interference, but feeling that there was sorrow and mourning behind for him even then—that his trust in man had been cruelly bruised. *The lots declared that Silas Marner was guilty.* He was solemnly suspended from church-membership, and called upon to render up the stolen money:

SIMON VAN BOOY

only on confession, as the sign of repentance, could he be received once more within the fold of the church. Marner listened in silence. At last, when every one rose to depart, he went towards William Dane and said, in a voice shaken by agitation—

"The last time I remember using my knife, was when I took it out to cut a strap for you. I don't remember putting it in my pocket again. *You* stole the money, and you have woven a plot to lay the sin at my door. But you may prosper, for all that: there is no just God that governs the earth righteously, but a God of lies, that bears witness against the innocent."

There was a general shudder at this blasphemy.

William said meekly, "I leave our brethren to judge whether this is the voice of Satan or not. I can do nothing but pray for you, Silas."

Poor Marner went out with that despair in his soul—that shaken trust in God and man, which is little short of madness to a loving nature. In the bitterness of his wounded spirit, he said to himself, "*She* will cast me off too." And he reflected that, if she did not believe the testimony against him, her whole faith must be upset as his was. To people accustomed to reason about the forms in which their religious feeling has incorporated itself, it is difficult to enter into that simple, untaught state of mind in which the form and the feeling have never been severed by an act of reflection. We are apt to think it inevitable that a man in Marner's position should have begun to question the validity of an appeal to the divine judgment by drawing lots; but to him this would have been an effort of independent thought such as he had never known; and he must have made the effort at a moment when all his energies were turned into the anguish of disappointed faith. If there is an angel who records the sorrows of men as well as their sins, he knows how many and deep are the sorrows that spring from false ideas for which no man is culpable.

Marner went home, and for a whole day sat alone, stunned by despair, without any impulse to go to Sarah and attempt to win her belief in his innocence. The second day he took refuge from benumbing unbelief, by getting into his loom and working away as usual; and before many hours were past, the minister and one of the deacons came to him with the message from Sarah, that she held her engagement to him at an end. Silas received the message mutely, and then turned away from the messengers to work at his loom again. In little more than a month from that time, Sarah was married to William Dane; and not long afterwards it was known to the brethren in Lantern Yard that Silas Marner had departed from the town.

She had set out at an early hour, but had lingered on the road, inclined by her indolence to believe that if she waited under

SIMON VAN BOOY

a warm shed the snow would cease to fall. She had waited longer than she knew, and now that she found herself belated in the snow-hidden ruggedness of the long lanes, even the animation of a vindictive purpose could not keep her spirit from failing. It was seven o'clock, and by this time she was not very far from Raveloe, but she was not familiar enough with those monotonous lanes to know how near she was to her journey's end. She needed comfort, and she knew but one comforter—the familiar demon in her bosom; but she hesitated a moment, after drawing out the black remnant, before she raised it to her lips. In that moment the mother's love pleaded for painful consciousness rather than oblivion—pleaded to be left in aching weariness, rather than to have the encircling arms benumbed so that they could not feel the dear burden. In another moment Molly had flung something away, but it was not the black remnant—it was an empty phial. And she walked on again under the breaking cloud, from which there came now and then the light of a quickly veiled star, for a freezing wind had sprung up since the snowing had ceased. But she walked always more and more drowsily, and clutched more and more automatically the sleeping child at her bosom.

Slowly the demon was working his will, and cold and weariness were his helpers. Soon she felt nothing but a supreme immediate longing that curtained off all futurity—the longing to lie down and sleep. She had arrived at a spot where her footsteps were no longer checked by a hedgerow, and she had wandered vaguely, unable to distinguish any objects, notwithstanding the wide whiteness around her, and the growing starlight. She sank down against a straggling furze bush, an easy pillow enough; and the bed of snow, too, was soft. She did not feel that the bed was cold, and did not heed whether the child would wake and cry for her. But her arms had not yet relaxed their instinctive clutch; and the little one slumbered on as gently as if it had been rocked in a lace-trimmed cradle.

But the complete torpor came at last: the fingers lost their tension, the arms unbent; then the little head fell away from the bosom, and the blue eyes opened wide on the cold starlight. At first there was a little peevish cry of "mammy," and an effort to regain the pillowing arm and bosom; but mammy's ear was deaf, and the pillow seemed to be slipping away backward. Suddenly, as the child rolled downward on its mother's knees, all wet with snow, its eyes were caught by a bright glancing light on the white ground, and, with the ready transition of infancy, it was immediately absorbed in watching the bright living thing running towards it, yet never arriving. That bright living thing must be caught; and in a instant the child had slipped on all fours, and held out one little hand to catch the gleam. But the gleam would not be caught in that way, and now the head was held up to see where the cunning

SIMON VAN BOOY

gleam came from. It came from a very bright place; and the little one, rising on its legs, toddled through the snow, the old grimy shawl in which it was wrapped trailing behind it, and the queer little bonnet dangling at its back—toddled on to the open door of Silas Marner's cottage, and right up to the warm hearth, where there was a bright fire of logs and sticks, which had thoroughly warmed the old sack (Silas's greatcoat) spread out on the bricks to dry. The little one, accustomed to be left to itself for long hours without notice from its mother, squatted down on the sack, and spread its tiny hands towards the blaze, in perfect contentment, gurgling and making many inarticulate communications to the cheerful fire, like a new-hatched gosling beginning to find itself comfortable. But presently the warmth had a lulling effect, and the little golden head sank down on the old sack, and the blue eyes were veiled by their delicate half-transparent lids.

But where was Silas Marner while this strange visitor had come to his hearth? He was in the cottage, but he did not see the child. During the last few weeks, since he had lost his money, he had contracted the habit of opening his door and looking out from time to time, as if he thought that his money might be somehow coming back to him, or that some trace, some news of it, might be mysteriously on the road, and be caught by the listening ear or the straining eye. It was chiefly at night, when he was not occupied in his loom, that he fell into this repetition of an act for which he could have assigned no definite purpose, and which can hardly be understood except by those who have undergone a bewildering separation from a supremely loved object. In the evening twilight, and later whenever the night was not dark, Silas looked out on that narrow prospect round the Stone-pits, listening and gazing, not with hope, but with mere yearning and unrest.

This morning he had been told by some of his neighbours that it was New Year's Eve, and that he must sit up and hear the old year rung out and the new rung in, because that was good luck, and might bring his money back again. This was only a friendly Raveloe-way of jesting with the half-crazy oddities of a miser, but it had perhaps helped to throw Silas into a more than usually excited state. Since the on-coming of twilight he had opened his door again and again, though only to shut it immediately at seeing all distance veiled by the falling snow. But the last time he opened it the snow had ceased, and the clouds were parting here and there. He stood and listened, and gazed for a long while—there was really something on the road coming towards him then, but he caught no sign of it; and the stillness and the wide trackless snow seemed to narrow his solitude, and touched his yearning with the chill of despair. He went in again, and put his right hand on the latch of the door to close it—but he did not close it: he was arrested, as he had been already since

SIMON VAN BOOY

his loss, by the invisible wand of catalepsy, and stood like a graven image, with wide but sightless eyes, holding open his door, powerless to resist either the good or evil that might enter there.

When Marner's sensibility returned, he continued the action which had been arrested, and closed his door, unaware of the chasm in his consciousness, unaware of any intermediate change, except that the light had grown dim, and that he was chilled and faint. He thought he had been too long standing at the door and looking out. Turning towards the hearth, where the two logs had fallen apart, and sent forth only a red uncertain glimmer, he seated himself on his fireside chair, and was stooping to push his logs together, when, to his blurred vision, it seemed as if there were gold on the floor in front of the hearth. Gold!—his own gold—brought back to him as mysteriously as it had been taken away! He felt his heart begin to beat violently, and for a few moments he was unable to stretch out his hand and grasp the restored treasure. The heap of gold seemed to glow and get larger beneath his agitated gaze. He leaned forward at last, and stretched forth his hand; but instead of the hard coin with the familiar resisting outline, his fingers encountered soft warm curls. In utter amazement, Silas fell on his knees and bent his head low to examine the marvel: it was a sleeping child—a round, fair thing, with soft yellow rings all over its head. Could this be his little sister come back to him in a dream—his little sister whom he had carried about in his arms for a year before she died, when he was a small boy without shoes or stockings? That was the first thought that darted across Sila's blank wonderment. *Was* it a dream? He rose to his feet again, pushed his logs together, and, throwing on some dried leaves and sticks, raised a flame; but the flame did not disperse the vision—it only lit up more distinctly the little round form of the child, and its shabby clothing. It was very much like his little sister. Silas sank into his chair, powerless under the double presence of an inexplicable surprise and a hurrying influx of memories. How and when had the child come in without his knowledge? He had never been beyond the door. But along with that question, and almost thrusting it away, there was a vision of the old home and the old streets leading to Lantern Yard—and within that vision another, of the thoughts which had been present with him in those far-off scenes. The thoughts were strange to him now, like old friendships impossible to revive; and yet he had a dreamy feeling that this child was somehow a message come to him from that far-off life: it stirred fibres that had never been moved in Raveloe—old quiverings of tenderness—old impressions of awe at the presentiment of some Power presiding over his life; for his imagination had not yet extricated itself from the sense of mystery in the child's sudden presence, and had formed no conjectures of ordinary

SIMON VAN BOOY

natural means by which the event could have been brought about.

But there was a cry on the hearth: the child had awaked, and Marner stooped to lift it on his knee. It clung round his neck, and burst louder and louder into that mingling of inarticulate cries with "mammy" by which little children express the bewilderment of waking. Silas pressed it to him, and almost unconsciously uttered sounds of hushing tenderness, while he bethought himself that some of his porridge, which had got cool by the dying fire, would do to feed the child with if it were only warmed up a little.

He had plenty to do through the next hour. The porridge, sweetened with some dry brown sugar from an old store which he had refrained from using for himself, stopped the cries of the little one, and made her lift her blue eyes with a wide quiet gaze at Silas, as he put the spoon into her mouth. Presently she slipped from his knee and began to toddle about, but with a pretty stagger that made Silas jump up and follow her lest she should fall against anything that would hurt her. But she only fell in a sitting posture on the ground, and began to pull at her boots, looking up at him with a crying face as if the boots hurt her. He took her on his knee again, but it was some time before it occurred to Silas's dull bachelor mind that the wet boots were the grievance, pressing on her warm ankles. He got them off with difficulty, and Baby was at once happily occupied with the primary mystery of her own toes, inviting Silas, with much chuckling, to consider the mystery too. But the wet boots had at last suggested to Silas that the child had been walking on the snow, and this roused him from his entire oblivion of any ordinary means by which it could have entered or been brought into his house. Under the prompting of this new idea, and without waiting to form conjectures, he raised the child in his arms, and went to the door. As soon as he had opened it, there was the cry of "mammy" again, which Silas had not heard since the child's first hungry waking. Bending forward, he could just discern the marks made by the little feet on the virgin snow, and he followed their track to the furze bushes. "Mammy!" the little one cried again and again, stretching itself forward so as almost to escape from Silas's arms, before he himself was aware that there was something more than the bush before him—that there was a human body, with the head sunk low in the furze, and half-covered with the shaken snow.

It was after the early supper-time at the Red House, and the entertainment was in that stage when bashfulness itself had passed into easy jollity, when gentlemen, conscious of unusual accomplishments, could at length be prevailed on to dance a hornpipe, and when the Squire preferred talking loudly, scattering snuff, and patting his visitors' backs, to sitting longer at the whist-table—a choice exasperating to uncle Kimble, who, being always volatile in sober business hours, became intense and bitter over cards and brandy, shuffled before his adversary's deal with a glare of suspicion, and turned up a mean trump-card with an air of inexpressible disgust, as if in a world where such things could happen one might as well enter on a course of reckless profligacy. When the evening had advanced to this pitch of freedom and enjoyment, it was usual for the servants, the heavy duties of supper being well over, to get their share of amusement by coming to look on at the dancing; so that the back regions of the house were left in solitude.

There were two doors by which the White Parlour was entered from the hall, and they were both standing open for the sake of air; but the lower one was crowded with the servants and villagers, and only the upper doorway was left free. Bob Cass was figuring in a hornpipe, and his father, very proud of this lithe son, whom he repeatedly declared to be just like himself in his young days in a tone that implied this to be the very highest stamp of juvenile merit, was the centre of a group who had placed themselves opposite the performer, not far from the upper door. Godfrey was standing a little way off, not to admire his brother's dancing, but to keep sight of Nancy, who was seated in the group, near her father. He stood aloof, because he wished to avoid suggesting himself as a subject for the Squire's fatherly jokes in connection with matrimony and Miss Nancy Lammeter's beauty, which were likely to become more and more explicit. But he had the prospect of dancing with her again when the hornpipe was concluded, and in the meanwhile it was very pleasant to get long glances at her quite unobserved.

But when Godfrey was lifting his eyes from one of those long glances, they encountered an object as startling to him at that moment as if it had been an apparition from the dead. It *was* an apparition from that hidden life which lies, like a dark by-street, behind the goodly ornamented façade that meets the sunlight and the gaze of respectable admirers. It was his own child carried in Silas Marner's arms. That was his instantaneous impression, unaccompanied by doubt, though he had not seen the child for months past; and when the hope was rising that he might possibly be mistaken, Mr. Crackenthorp and Mr. Lammeter had already advanced to Silas, in astonishment at this strange advent. Godfrey joined them immediately, unable to rest without hearing every word—trying to control himself, but conscious that if any one noticed him, they must see that he was white-lipped and trembling.

But now all eyes at that end of the room were bent on Silas Marner; the Squire himself had risen, and asked angrily, "How's this?—what's this?—what do you do coming in here in this way?"

"I'm come for the doctor—I want the doctor," Silas had said, in the first moment, to Mr. Crackenthorp.

"Why, what's the matter, Marner?" said the rector. "The doctor's here; but say quietly what you want him for."

"It's a woman," said Silas, speaking low, and half-breathlessly, just as Godfrey came up. "She's dead, I think—dead in the snow at the Stone-pits—not far from my door."

Godfrey felt a great throb: there was one terror in his mind at that moment: it was, that the woman might *not* be dead. That was an evil terror—an ugly inmate to have found a nestling-place in Godfrey's kindly disposition; but no disposition is a security from evil wishes to a man whose happiness hangs on duplicity.

"Hush, hush!" said Mr. Crackenthorp. "Go out into the hall there. I'll fetch the doctor to you. Found a woman in the snow—and thinks she's dead," he added, speaking low, to the Squire. "Better say as little about it as possible: it will shock the ladies. Just tell them a poor woman is ill from cold and hunger. I'll go and fetch Kimble."

By this time, however, the ladies had pressed forward, curious to know what could have brought the solitary linen-weaver there under such strange circumstances, and interested in the pretty child, who, half alarmed and half attracted by the brightness and the numerous company, now frowned and hid her face, now lifted up her head again and looked round placably, until a touch or a coaxing word brought back the frown, and made her bury her face with new determination.

"What child is it?" said several ladies at once, and, among the rest, Nancy Lammeter, addressing Godfrey.

"I don't know—some poor woman's who has been found in the snow, I believe," was the answer Godfrey wrung from himself with a terrible effort. ("After all, *am* I certain?" he hastened to add, in anticipation of his own conscience.)

"Why, you'd better leave the child here, then, Master Marner," said good-natured Mrs. Kimble, hesitating, however, to take those dingy clothes into contact with her own ornamented satin boddice. "I'll tell one o' the girls to fetch it."

"No—no—I can't part with it, I can't let it go," said Silas, abruptly. "It's come to me—I've a right to keep it."

The proposition to take the child from him had come to Silas quite unexpectedly, and his speech, uttered under a strong sudden impulse, was almost like a revelation to himself: a minute before, he had no distinct intention about the child.

"Did you ever hear the like?" said Mrs. Kimble, in mild surprise, to her neighbor.

"Now, ladies, I must trouble you to stand aside," said Mr. Kimble, coming from the card-room, in some bitterness at the interruption, but drilled by the long habit of his profession into obedience to unpleasant calls, even when he was hardly sober.

"It's a nasty business turning out now, eh, Kimble?" said

SIMON VAN BOOY

the Squire. "He might ha' gone for your young fellow—the 'prentice, there—what's his name?"

"Might? ay—what's the use of talking about might?" growled uncle Kimble, hastening out with Marner, and followed by Mr. Crackenthorp and Godfrey. "Get me a pair of thick boots, Godfrey, will you? And stay, let somebody run to Winthrop's and fetch Dolly—she's the best woman to get. Ben was here himself before supper; is he gone?"

"Yes, sir, I met him," said Marner; "but I couldn't stop to tell him anything, only I said I was going for the doctor, and he said the doctor was at the Squire's. And I made haste and ran, and there was nobody to be seen at the back o' the house, and so I went in to where the company was."

The child, no longer distracted by the bright light and the smiling women's faces, began to cry and call for "mammy," though always clinging to Marner, who had apparently won her thorough confidence. Godfrey had come back with the boots, and felt the cry as if some fibre were drawn tight within him.

"I'll go," he said, hastily, eager for some movement; "I'll go and fetch the woman—Mrs. Winthrop."

"Oh, pooh—send somebody else," said uncle Kimble, hurrying away with Marner.

"You'll let me know if I can be of any use, Kimble," said Mr. Crackenthorp. But the doctor was out of hearing.

Godfrey, too, had disappeared: he was gone to snatch his hat and coat, having just reflection enough to remember that he must not look like a madman; but he rushed out of the house into the snow without heeding his thin shoes.

In a few minutes he was on his rapid way to the Stone-pits by the side of Dolly, who, though feeling that she was entirely in her place in encountering cold and snow on an errand of mercy, was much concerned at a young gentleman's getting his feet wet under a like impulse.

"You'd a deal better go back, sir," said Dolly, with respectful compassion. "You've no call to catch cold; and I'd ask you if you'd be so good as tell my husband to come, on your way back—he's at the Rainbow, I doubt—if you found him anyway sober enough to be o' use. Or else, there's Mrs. Snell 'ud happen send the boy up to fetch and carry, for there may be things wanted from the doctor's."

"No, I'll stay, now I'm once out—I'll stay outside here," said Godfrey, when they came opposite Marner's cottage. "You can come and tell me if I can do anything."

"Well, sir, you're very good: you've a tender heart," said Dolly, going to the door.

Godfrey was too painfully preoccupied to feel a twinge of self-reproach at this undeserved praise. He walked up and down, unconscious that he was plunging ankle-deep in snow, unconscious of everything but trembling suspense about what was going on in the cottage, and the effect of each alternative on his future lot. No, not quite unconscious of everything else. Deeper down, and half-smothered by passionate desire and dread, there was the sense that he ought not to be waiting on these alternatives; that he ought to accept the consequences of his deeds, own the miserable wife, and fulfil the claims of the helpless child. But he had not moral courage enough to contemplate that active renunciation of Nancy as possible for him: he had only conscience and heart enough to make him forever uneasy under the weakness that forbade the renunciation. And at this moment his mind leaped away from all restraint towards the sudden prospect of deliverance from his long bondage.

"Is she dead?" said the voice that predominated over every other within him. "If she is, I may marry Nancy; and then I shall be a good fellow in future, and have no secrets, and the child— shall be taken care of somehow." But across that vision came the other possibility—"She may live, and then it's all up with me."

Godfrey never knew how long it was before the door of the cottage opened and Mr. Kimble came out. He went forward to meet his uncle, prepared to suppress the agitation he must feel, whatever news he was to hear.

"I waited for you, as I'd come so far," he said, speaking first.

"Pooh, it was nonsense for you to come out: why didn't you send one of the men? There's nothing to be done. She's dead—has been dead for hours, I should say."

"What sort of woman is she?" said Godfrey, feeling the blood rush to his face.

"A young woman, but emaciated, with long black hair. Some vagrant—quite in rags. She's got a wedding-ring on, however. They must fetch her away to the workhouse to-morrow. Come, come along."

"I want to look at her," said Godfrey. "I think I saw such a woman yesterday. I'll overtake you in a minute or two."

Mr. Kimble went on, and Godfrey turned back to the cottage. He cast only one glance at the dead face on the pillow, which Dolly had smoothed with decent care; but he remembered that last look at his unhappy hated wife so well, that at the end of sixteen years every line in the worn face was present to him when he told the full story of this night.

He turned immediately towards the hearth, where Silas Marner sat lulling the child. She was perfectly quiet now, but not asleep—only soothed by sweet porridge and warmth into that wide-gazing calm which makes us older human beings, with our inward turmoil, feel a certain awe in the presence of a little child, such as we feel before some quiet majesty or beauty in the earth or sky—before a steady glowing planet, or a full-flowered eglantine, or the bending trees over a silent pathway. The wide-open blue eyes looked up at Godfrey's without any uneasiness or sign of recognition: the child could make no visible [or] audible claim on its father; and the father felt a strange mixture of feelings, a conflict of regret and joy, that the pulse of that little heart had no response for the half-jealous yearning in his own, when the blue eyes turned away from him slowly, and fixed themselves on the weaver's queer face, which was bent low down to look at them, while the small hand began to pull Marner's withered cheek with loving disfiguration.

"You'll take the child to the parish tomorrow?" asked Godfrey, speaking as indifferently as he could.

"Who says so?" said Marner, sharply. "Will they make me take her?"

"Why, you wouldn't like to keep her, should you—an old bachelor like you?"

"Till anybody shows they've a right to take her away from me," said Marner. "The mother's dead, and I reckon it's got no father: it's a lone thing—and I'm a lone thing."

Mary Cassat, *The Bath*, 1893

Poet and artist Adrian Henri was influenced by French symbolism, but also the pop culture of 1960s Liverpool, which many readers believe made his poetry more accessible to a younger audience. Henri grew up in Rhyl, North Wales, but studied art at Newcastle. In the 1970s, he was made an honorary professor of John Moores University, and maintained close friendships with other influential artists of his generation, including Allen Ginsberg, John Lennon, and Roger McGough. He married twice, but didn't have any children. He died in 2000 after a long illness.

His poem "Without You" is a humorous tribute to how love has brought meaning to the narrator's life.

Adrian Henri

"Without You"

Without you every morning would be like going back to work
   after a holiday,
Without you I couldn't stand the smell of the East Lancs Road,
Without you ghost ferries would cross the Mersey manned by
   skeleton crews,
Without you I'd probably feel happy and have more money
   and time and nothing to do with it,
Without you I'd have to leave my stillborn poems on other
   people's doorsteps, wrapped in brown paper,
Without you there'd never be sauce to put on sausage butties,
Without you plastic flowers in shop windows would just be
   plastic flowers in shop windows
Without you I'd spend my summers picking morosely over the
   remains of train crashes,
Without you white birds would wrench themselves free from
   my paintings and fly off dripping blood into the night,
Without you green apples wouldn't taste greener,
Without you Mothers wouldn't let their children play out
   after tea,
Without you every musician in the world would forget how to
   play the blues,
Without you Public Houses would be public again,

SIMON VAN BOOY

Without you the Sunday Times colour supplement would
come out in black-and-white,
Without you indifferent colonels would shrug their shoulders
and press the button,
Without you they'd stop changing the flowers in Piccadilly
Gardens,
Without you Clark Kent would forget how to become
Superman,
Without you Sunshine Breakfast would only consist of
Cornflakes,
Without you there'd be no colour in Magic colouring books
Without you Mahler's 8th would only be performed by street
musicians in derelict houses,
Without you they'd forget to put the salt in every packet of
crisps,
Without you it would be an offence punishable by a fine of up
to £200 or two months imprisonment to be found in
possession of curry powder,
Without you riot police are massing in quiet sidestreets,
Without you all streets would be one-way the other way,
Without you there'd be no one not to kiss goodnight when we
quarrel,
Without you the first martian to land would turn round and go
away again,
Without you they'd forget to change the weather,

Without you blind men would sell unlucky heather,
Without you there would be
no landscapes/no stations/no houses,
no chipshops/no quiet villages/no seagulls
on beaches/no hopscotch on pavements/no
night/no morning/there'd be no city no country
Without you.

William Blake was a visionary poet and painter who lived in Britain in the late 1700s. He was largely unappreciated and misunderstood during his lifetime. One of Blake's contemporaries even referred to him as a harmless lunatic. Blake spent his life not only as a dedicated husband and well-regarded engraver but also as a kind of mystic—claiming to receive messages from the dead and see ghosts. Modern scholars consider Blake to be a genius, and modern students often find his work puzzling.

Blake wrote and illustrated his own poetry books, using the same skills in his profession as an engraver. When Blake died, he was buried in an unmarked grave at a public cemetery in London. After his death, the English poet William Wordsworth remarked that "There was no doubt that this poor man was mad, but there is something in the madness of this man which interests me more than the sanity of Lord Byron and Walter Scott."

This early Blake poem represents opposite ideas of love, as expressed by two characters in very different physical circumstances.

William Blake

"The Clod and the Pebble"

Love seeketh not Itself to please,
Nor for itself hath any care;
But for another gives its ease,
And builds a Heaven in Hell's despair.

So sang a little Clod of Clay,
Trodden with the cattle's feet:
But a pebble of the brook,
Warbled out these metres meet.

Love seeketh only Self to please,
To bind another to Its delight:
Joys in another's loss of ease,
And builds a Hell in Heaven's despite.

Who, being loved, is poor?

—*Oscar Wilde*

William Sydney Porter was born in Greensboro, North Carolina. In 1887 at age twenty-five, he married Athol Estes. Seven years into the marriage, Porter was accused of embezzlement at the bank where he worked and lost his job. Soon after, he fled to Honduras, while his family moved into his wife's family home. When he returned to the United States in 1897 to visit his wife on her deathbed, Porter was quickly arrested and sentenced to five years in prison. While in prison, Porter had many stories published under pseudonyms, but was best known as O. Henry. After serving three years, Porter was released and moved to New York City with his eleven-year-old daughter, where he wrote prolifically to support her. He died in 1910.

"The Gift of the Magi" echoes the sentiment of the Blake poem—that love can beautify the world by helping us overcome the selfishness that limits our experience of love.

O. Henry

"The Gift of the Magi"

One dollar and eighty-seven cents. That was all. And sixty cents of it was in pennies. Pennies saved one and two at a time by bulldozing the grocer and the vegetable man and the butcher until one's cheeks burned with the silent imputation of parsimony that such close dealing implied. Three times Della counted it. One dollar and eighty-seven cents. And the next day would be Christmas.

There was clearly nothing to do but flop down on the shabby little couch and howl. So Della did it. Which instigates the moral reflection that life is made up of sobs, sniffles, and smiles, with sniffles predominating.

While the mistress of the home is gradually subsiding from the first stage to the second, take a look at the home. A furnished flat at $8 per week. It did not exactly beggar description, but it certainly had that word on the lookout for the mendicancy squad.

In the vestibule below was a letter-box into which no letter would go, and an electric button from which no mortal finger could coax a ring. Also appertaining thereunto was a card bearing the name "Mr. James Dillingham Young."

The "Dillingham" had been flung to the breeze during a former period of prosperity when its possessor was being paid $30 per week. Now, when the income was shrunk to $20, though, they were thinking seriously of contracting to a modest and unassuming D. But whenever Mr. James Dillingham Young came home and reached his flat above he was called "Jim" and greatly hugged by Mrs. James Dillingham Young, already introduced to you as Della. Which is all very good.

Della finished her cry and attended to her cheeks with the powder rag. She stood by the window and looked out dully at a gray cat walking a gray fence in a gray backyard. Tomorrow would be Christmas Day, and she had only $1.87 with which to buy Jim a present. She had been saving every penny she could for months, with this result. Twenty dollars a week doesn't go far. Expenses had been greater than she had calculated. They always are. Only $1.87 to buy a present for Jim. Her Jim. Many a happy hour she had spent planning for something nice for him. Something fine and rare and sterling—something just a little bit near to being worthy of the honor of being owned by Jim.

There was a pier-glass between the windows of the room. Perhaps you have seen a pier-glass in an $8 flat. A very thin and very agile person may, by observing his reflection in a rapid sequence of longitudinal strips, obtain a fairly accurate conception of his looks. Della, being slender, had mastered the art.

Suddenly she whirled from the window and stood before the glass. Her eyes were shining brilliantly, but her face had lost its color within twenty seconds. Rapidly she pulled down her hair and let it fall to its full length.

Now, there were two possessions of the James Dillingham Youngs in which they both took a mighty pride. One was Jim's gold watch that had been his father's and his grandfather's. The other was Della's hair. Had the queen of Sheba lived in the flat across the airshaft, Della would have let her hair hang out the window some day to dry just to depreciate Her Majesty's jewels and gifts. Had King Solomon been the janitor, with all his treasures piled up in the basement, Jim would have pulled out his watch every time he passed, just to see him pluck at his beard from envy.

So now Della's beautiful hair fell about her rippling and shining like a cascade of brown waters. It reached below her knee and made itself almost a garment for her. And then she did it up again nervously and quickly. Once she faltered for a minute and stood still while a tear or two splashed on the worn red carpet.

On went her old brown jacket; on went her old brown hat. With a whirl of skirts and with the brilliant sparkle still in her eyes, she fluttered out the door and down the stairs to the street. Where she stopped the sign read: "Mme. Sofronie. Hair Goods of All Kinds." One flight up Della ran, and collected herself, panting. Madame, large, too white, chilly, hardly looked the "Sofronie."

"Will you buy my hair?" asked Della.

"I buy hair," said Madame. "Take yer hat off and let's have a sight at the looks of it."

Down rippled the brown cascade.

"Twenty dollars," said Madame, lifting the mass with a practised hand.

"Give it to me quick," said Della.

Oh, and the next two hours tripped by on rosy wings. Forget the hashed metaphor. She was ransacking the stores for Jim's present.

She found it at last. It surely had been made for Jim and no one else. There was no other like it in any of the stores, and she had turned all of them inside out. It was a platinum fob chain simple and chaste in design, properly proclaiming its value by substance alone and not by meretricious ornamentation—as all good things should do. It was even worthy of The Watch. As soon as she saw it she knew that it must be Jim's. It was like him. Quietness and value—the description applied to both. Twenty-one dollars they took from her for it, and she hurried home with the 87 cents. With that chain on his watch Jim might be properly anxious about the time in any company. Grand as the watch was, he sometimes looked at it on the sly on account of the old leather strap that he used in place of a chain.

When Della reached home her intoxication gave way a

little to prudence and reason. She got out her curling irons and lighted the gas and went to work repairing the ravages made by generosity added to love. Which is always a tremendous task, dear friends—a mammoth task.

Within forty minutes her head was covered with tiny, close-lying curls that made her look wonderfully like a truant schoolboy. She looked at her reflection in the mirror long, carefully, and critically.

"If Jim doesn't kill me," she said to herself, "before he takes a second look at me, he'll say I look like a Coney Island chorus girl. But what could I do—oh! what could I do with a dollar and eighty-seven cents?"

At 7 o'clock the coffee was made and the frying-pan was on the back of the stove hot and ready to cook the chops.

Jim was never late. Della doubled the fob chain in her hand and sat on the corner of the table near the door that he always entered. Then she heard his step on the stair away down on the first flight, and she turned white for just a moment. She had a habit for saying a little silent prayer about the simplest everyday things, and now she whispered: "Please God, make him think I am still pretty."

The door opened and Jim stepped in and closed it. He looked thin and very serious. Poor fellow, he was only twenty-two—and to be burdened with a family! He needed a new overcoat and he was without gloves.

Jim stopped inside the door, as immovable as a setter at the scent of quail. His eyes were fixed upon Della, and there was an expression in them that she could not read, and it terrified her. It was not anger, nor surprise, nor disapproval, nor horror, nor any of the sentiments that she had been prepared for. He simply stared at her fixedly with that peculiar expression on his face. Della wriggled off the table and went for him.

"Jim, darling," she cried, "don't look at me that way. I had my hair cut off and sold because I couldn't have lived through Christmas without giving you a present. It'll grow out again— you won't mind, will you? I just had to do it. My hair grows awfully fast. Say 'Merry Christmas!' Jim, and let's be happy. You don't know what a nice—what a beautiful, nice gift I've got for you."

"You've cut off your hair?" asked Jim, laboriously, as if he had not arrived at that patent fact yet even after the hardest mental labor.

"Cut it off and sold it," said Della. "Don't you like me just as well, anyhow? I'm me without my hair, ain't I?"

Jim looked about the room curiously.

"You say your hair is gone?" he said, with an air almost of idiocy.

"You needn't look for it," said Della. "It's sold, I tell you— sold and gone, too. It's Christmas Eve, boy. Be good to me, for it went for you. Maybe the hairs of my head were numbered," she went on with sudden serious sweetness, "but nobody could ever count my love for you. Shall I put the chops on, Jim?"

Out of his trance Jim seemed quickly to wake. He enfolded his Della. For ten seconds let us regard with discreet scrutiny some inconsequential object in the other direction. Eight dollars a week or a million a year—what is the difference? A mathematician or a wit would give you the wrong answer. The magi brought valuable gifts, but that was not among them. This dark assertion will be illuminated later on.

Jim drew a package from his overcoat pocket and threw it upon the table.

"Don't make any mistake, Dell," he said, "about me. I don't think there's anything in the way of a haircut or a shave or a shampoo that could make me like my girl any less. But if you'll unwrap that package you may see why you had me going a while at first."

White fingers and nimble tore at the string and paper. And then an ecstatic scream of joy; and then, alas! a quick feminine change to hysterical tears and wails, necessitating the immediate employment of all the comforting powers of the lord of the flat.

For there lay The Combs—the set of combs, side and back, that Della had worshipped long in a Broadway window. Beautiful combs, pure tortoise shell, with jewelled rims—just the shade to wear in the beautiful vanished hair. They were expensive combs, she knew, and her heart had simply craved and yearned over them without the least hope of possession. And now, they were hers, but the tresses that should have adorned the coveted adornments were gone.

But she hugged them to her bosom, and at length she was able to look up with dim eyes and a smile and say: "My hair grows so fast, Jim!"

And then Della leaped up like a little singed cat and cried, "Oh, oh!"

Jim had not yet seen his beautiful present. She held it out to him eagerly upon her open palm. The dull precious metal seemed to flash with a reflection of her bright and ardent spirit.

"Isn't it a dandy, Jim? I hunted all over town to find it. You'll have to look at the time a hundred times a day now. Give me your watch. I want to see how it looks on it."

Instead of obeying, Jim tumbled down on the couch and put his hands under the back of his head and smiled.

"Dell," said he, "let's put our Christmas presents away and keep 'em a while. They're too nice to use just at present. I sold the watch to get the money to buy your combs. And now suppose you put the chops on."

The magi, as you know, were wise men—wonderfully wise men—who brought gifts to the Babe in the manger. They invented the art of giving Christmas presents. Being wise, their gifts were no doubt wise ones, possibly bearing the privilege of exchange in case of duplication. And here I have lamely related to you the uneventful chronicle of two foolish children in a flat who most unwisely sacrificed for each other the greatest treasures of their house. But in a last word to the wise of these days let it be said that of all who give gifts these two were the wisest. O all who give and receive gifts, such as they are wisest. Everywhere they are wisest. They are the magi.

Noor Inayat Khan was born in Moscow in 1914 to an American father and Indian mother. She spent a large part of her childhood in Paris and studied at two of Europe's most prestigious schools, the Sorbonne and the Paris Conservatory. In 1939, as Nazi troops invaded Poland, Khan's book *Twenty Jataka Tales* was being published in London.

During World War II she worked as a British secret agent. She was captured in 1943 and executed by the Nazis in 1944, aged thirty.

These stories (retold by Khan) are roughly 2,500 years old and reflect the Buddhist tradition in literature, where kindness, self-sacrifice, charity, and nonviolence are often used to solve conflict.

Noor Inayat Khan

"The Kind Elephant" from *Twenty Jataka Tales*

Far, far in the sandy desert was a small oasis of palm trees and flowers. And in that oasis, as a lonely hermit, lived an elephant, a beautiful elephant. He ate the fruit of the trees, and drank from a little stream of water that ran through the rocks. Happy he was, dancing through the banana trees, watching day and night come over the desert.

But one day, as he was dancing along, in the distance some strange voices came to his ears.

"Whose are those voices?" he said to himself. "Are they not voices of men, of unhappy men? Who are those men, and why do they cross the desert? Surely they are lost, or maybe they suffer some terrible pain."

Such were the thoughts of the handsome elephant as he walked in the direction of the voices. He walked some distance over the burning sand when he came upon a great crowd of men all huddled together at death's door, and at the piteous sight his eyes, for the first time in his happy life, filled with tears.

"O travelers," he said to them in a tender voice, "wherefrom do you come, and where are you going? Have you lost your way in the desert? Tell me, O men, that I may help you in some way."

So happy were the men to hear these friendly words that they fell on their knees before him.

"Beautiful one," they said, "we have been driven from our country by our King, and have roamed through the desert for many days. Not a drop of water have we found to drink, nor food to give us strength."

"Help us, O dear one," they cried; "help us."

"How many are you?" asked the elephant.

"We were one thousand," they replied, "but many have perished on the way."

The elephant gazed at them. One was crying for water, another asking for food.

"You are weak, O men," he said, "and the next city is too far for you to reach without food and drink. Therefore walk towards the hill which stands before you. At its foot you will find the body of a large elephant which will provide you with food, and nearby runs a stream of sweet water."

When he had thus spoken he ran over the burning sand and disappeared as he had come.

"Where did the elephant go? And why did he run at such a pace?"

Straight to the hill he went, to the same hill he had pointed out to the men; but he took another way, that the men might not see him going. He climbed to the top of the hill and then from its highest point, in a mighty jump, his beautiful body crashed to the ground below.

When the men reached the spot they gazed at the giant-like form and a great fear seized them.

"Is this not our dear elephant?" exclaimed one among them.

"This face is the same face; the eyes, though closed, are the same eyes," said another.

And they all sat in the sand and wept bitterly.

After some time one among them spoke.

"Companions," he said, "we cannot eat this elephant who has given his life for us."

"Nay, friends," said another, "if we do not eat this elephant, his sacrifice will have been useless, and we shall die before reaching another city. Thus we shall not be helped, nor shall the wish of our elephant be fulfilled."

The men spoke no more but bent their heads in the burning sand and ate the meat with tears in their eyes. And it made them strong, very strong, so that they were able to cross the desert and reach a town where their troubles came to an end. They never forgot the great elephant, and they lived happily ever after.

SIMON VAN BOOY

It is impossible to obtain a conviction for sodomy from an English jury. Half of them don't believe that it can physically be done, and the other half are doing it.

—*Winston Churchill*

As wolves love lambs so lovers love their loves.

—*Plato*

Born in 1822, Mathew Arnold was a Victorian poet and critic. In addition to teaching, Arnold was also a school inspector, a job that enabled him to explore England extensively by rail. He married at twenty-nine years of age and had six children, three of whom died in their youth. Arnold died in 1888.

In the poem "Dover Beach," Arnold cries out to the redemptive power of love and personal fidelity in a world of dwindling religious faith.

Matthew Arnold

"Dover Beach"

The sea is calm tonight,
The tide is full, the moon lies fair
Upon the straits; on the French coast the light
Gleams and is gone; the cliffs of England stand,
Glimmering and vast, out in the tranquil bay.
Come to the window, sweet is the night air!
Only, from the long line of spray
Where the sea meets the moon-blanched land,
Listen! you hear the grating roar
Of pebbles which the waves draw back, and fling,
At their return, up the high strand,
Begin, and cease, and then again begin,
With tremulous cadence slow, and bring
The eternal note of sadness in.

Sophocles long ago
Heard it on the Aegean, and it brought
Into his mind the turbid ebb and flow
Of human misery; we
Find also in the sound a thought,
Hearing it by this distant northern sea.

The Sea of Faith

Was once, too, at the full, and round earth's shore

Lay like the folds of a bright girdle furled.

But now I only hear

Its melancholy, long, withdrawing roar,

Retreating, to the breath

Of the night wind, down the vast edges drear

And naked shingles of the world.

Ah, love, let us be true

To one another! for the world, which seems

To lie before us like a land of dreams,

So various, so beautiful, so new,

Hath really neither joy, nor love, nor light,

Nor certitude, nor peace, nor help for pain;

And we are here as on a darkling plain

Swept with confused alarms of struggle and flight,

Where ignorant armies clash by night.

Giovanni Battista Salvi da Sassoferrato was an Italian Baroque painter, born in the town of Sassoferrato in 1609. He specialized in religious images, and painted to order—often reproducing similar versions of the same painting. Very little is known about his life. He died in 1685.

In *The Virgin and Child Embracing*, the apotheosis of mother and child suggests that love is our connection to an immortal, spiritual realm that reaches beyond our own short lives.

Giovanni Battista Salvi da Sassoferrato, *The Virgin and Child Embracing,* 1660–85

Hafiz (born Shams-ud-din Muhammad) is one of Persia's most well-known poets. He was born in 1320 and lived during the same period as Chaucer in England. His musical wit, generosity, devotion to God, and reverence for beauty have helped to ensure this enormous success as a poet over the past several hundred years. He died in 1389, leaving around 5,000 poems, though only about 10 percent of his poetic work has survived.

Hafiz

"Throw Me On a Scale"

Today love has completely gutted me.
I am lying in the market like a
Filleted grouper,

Speechless,
Every desire and sinew absolutely silent
But I am still so fresh.

Everything is now the same to me.
Listen:

The touch of a beautiful woman
As she lifts me near,
Drawing my scent into her body;
She thinks about taking me home.

The touch of a wondrous fly
Drinking my vital fluids
Through a strange shaped flute,

The sun laying its radiant gaze against my cheek,
Human voices and the breeze from a passing
Horse's tail,

SIMON VAN BOOY

All send miraculous currents into
My world.

God's beauty has split me wide open.
Throw Hafiz on a scale,
Wrap me in cloth,
Bring me home.

Hafiz

"Two Giant Fat People"

God

And I have become

Like two giant fat people

Living in a

Tiny boat.

We

Keep

Bumping into each other and

L
a
u
g
h
i
n
g

SIMON VAN BOOY

Benvenuto Tisi da Garofalo was a late Renaissance Italian painter born in 1481, who is believed to have worked with Boccaccino, Raphael, and Dossa Dossi. Garofalo painted mostly in oil and in fresco, exploring religious subjects in paintings such as *Massacre of the Innocents* and *Betrayal of Christ*. He died in 1559.

In these two paintings, Saint Nicholas of Tolentino brings a child back to life, and in the second revives birds cooked for his lunch during an illness. This elegant pair of mid-sixteenth-century works illustrates how love and faith are, quite literally, more powerful than death.

Benvenuto Tisi da Garofalo, *Saint Nicholas of Tolentino Reviving a Child,* 1530

Benvenuto Tisi da Garofalo, *Saint Nicholas of Tolentino Reviving the Birds*, 1530

It is better to be hated for what you are than to be loved for something you are not.

—*Andre Gide*

Willa Cather was born in Virginia in 1873 and moved with her family to the pioneer state of Nebraska when she was nine. Thus began the experience that would characterize her most popular writing: the struggle of homesteaders and the rise of European immigrants in the North American west. Cather graduated from university in 1895 and spent most of her life as a writer—either for magazines or of books.

"Paul's Case" is the story of a unique teenage boy whose sensitive nature is at odds with the industrialized, capitalist city where he lives. Paul's mother seems to have died when he was young, and although it's clear that Paul's father loves him, he seems disappointed in his son—as though he sees only who his son *should* be, rather than who his son actually is. In this story, we are presented with a boy whose need for love is not the need for passion or constancy, but the need for understanding, for recognition, and for appreciation of who he actually is—and not for who others wish him to be.

Willa Cather

"Paul's Case: A Study in Temperament"

It was Paul's afternoon to appear before the faculty of the Pittsburgh High School to account for his various misdemeanours. He had been suspended a week ago, and his father had called at the Principal's office and confessed his perplexity about his son. Paul entered the faculty room suave and smiling. His clothes were a trifle out-grown and the tan velvet on the collar of his open overcoat was frayed and worn; but for all that there was something of the dandy about him, and he wore an opal pin in his neatly knotted black four-in-hand, and a red carnation in his buttonhole. This latter adornment the faculty somehow felt was not properly significant of the contrite spirit befitting a boy under the ban of suspension.

Paul was tall for his age and very thin, with high, cramped shoulders and a narrow chest. His eyes were remarkable for a certain hysterical brilliancy, and he continually used them in a conscious, theatrical sort of way, peculiarly offensive in a boy. The pupils were abnormally large, as though he were addicted to belladonna, but there was a glassy glitter about them which that drug does not produce.

When questioned by the Principal as to why he was there, Paul stated, politely enough, that he wanted to come back to school. This was a lie, but Paul was quite accustomed to lying;

found it, indeed, indispensable for overcoming friction. His teachers were asked to state their respective charges against him, which they did with such a rancour and aggrievedness as evinced that this was not a usual case. Disorder and impertinence were among the offences named, yet each of his instructors felt that it was scarcely possible to put into words the real cause of the trouble, which lay in a sort of hysterically defiant manner of the boy's; in the contempt which they all knew he felt for them, and which he seemingly made not the least effort to conceal. Once, when he had been making a synopsis of a paragraph at the blackboard, his English teacher had stepped to his side and attempted to guide his hand. Paul had started back with a shudder and thrust his hands violently behind him. The astonished woman could scarcely have been more hurt and embarrassed had he struck at her. The insult was so involuntary and definitely personal as to be unforgettable. In one way and another, he had made all his teachers, men and women alike, conscious of the same feeling of physical aversion. In one class he habitually sat with his hand shading his eyes; in another he always looked out of the window during the recitation; in another he made a running commentary on the lecture, with humorous intention.

His teachers felt this afternoon that his whole attitude was symbolized by his shrug and his flippantly red carnation flower, and they fell upon him without mercy, his English

SIMON VAN BOOY

teacher leading the pack. He stood through it smiling, his pale lips parted over his white teeth. (His lips were continually twitching, and he had a habit of raising his eyebrows that was contemptuous and irritating to the last degree.) Older boys than Paul had broken down and shed tears under that baptism of fire, but his set smile did not once desert him, and his only sign of discomfort was the nervous trembling of the fingers that toyed with the buttons of his overcoat, and an occasional jerking of the other hand that held his hat. Paul was always smiling, always glancing about him, seeming to feel that people might be watching him and trying to detect something. This conscious expression, since it was as far as possible from boyish mirthfulness, was usually attributed to insolence or "smartness."

As the inquisition proceeded, one of his instructors repeated an impertinent remark of the boy's, and the Principal asked him whether he thought that a courteous speech to have made a woman. Paul shrugged his shoulders slightly and his eyebrows twitched.

"I don't know," he replied. "I didn't mean to be polite or impolite, either. I guess it's a sort of way I have of saying things regardless."

The Principal, who was a sympathetic man, asked him whether he didn't think that a way it would be well to get rid of. Paul grinned and said he guessed so. When he was told that he could go, he bowed gracefully and went out: His bow was but a repetition of the scandalous red carnation.

His teachers were in despair, and his drawing master voiced the feeling of them all when he declared there was something about the boy which none of them understood. He added: "I don't really believe that smile of his comes altogether from insolence; there's something sort of haunted about it. The boy is not strong, for one thing. I happen to know that he was born in Colorado, only a few months before his mother died out there of a long illness. There is something wrong about the fellow."

The drawing master had come to realize that, in looking at Paul, one saw only his white teeth and the forced animation of his eyes. One warm afternoon the boy had gone to sleep at his drawing-board, and his master had noted with amazement what a white, blue-veined face it was; drawn and wrinkled like an old man's about the eyes, the lips twitching even in his sleep, and stiff with a nervous tension that drew them back from his teeth.

His teachers left the building dissatisfied and unhappy; humiliated to have felt so vindictive toward a mere boy, to have uttered this feeling in cutting terms, and to have set each other on, as it were, in the grew some game of intemperate reproach. Some of them remembered having seen a miserable street cat set at bay by a ring of tormentors.

SIMON VAN BOOY

As for Paul, he ran down the hill whistling the Soldiers' Chorus from *Faust* looking wildly behind him now and then to see whether some of his teachers were not there to writhe under his light-heartedness. As it was now late in the afternoon and Paul was on duty that evening as usher at Carnegie Hall, he decided that he would not go home to supper. When he reached the concert hall the doors were not yet open and, as it was chilly outside, he decided to go up into the picture gallery—always deserted at this hour—where there were some of Raffaelli's gay studies of Paris streets and an airy blue Venetian scene or two that always exhilarated him. He was delighted to find no one in the gallery but the old guard, who sat in one corner, a newspaper on his knee, a black patch over one eye and the other closed. Paul possessed himself of the place and walked confidently up and down, whistling under his breath. After a while he sat down before a blue Rico and lost himself. When he bethought him to look at his watch, it was after seven o'clock, and he rose with a start and ran downstairs, making a face at Augustus, peering out from the cast-room, and an evil gesture at the *Venus of Milo* as he passed her on the stairway.

When Paul reached the ushers' dressing-room half-a-dozen boys were there already, and he began excitedly to tumble into his uniform. It was one of the few that at all approached fitting, and Paul thought it very becoming—though he knew that the tight, straight coat accentuated his narrow chest, about which he was exceedingly sensitive. He was always considerably excited while he dressed, twanging all over to the tuning of the strings and the preliminary flourishes of the horns in the music-room; but tonight he seemed quite beside himself, and he teased and plagued the boys until, telling him that he was crazy, they put him down on the floor and sat on him.

Somewhat calmed by his suppression, Paul dashed out to the front of the house to seat the early comers. He was a model usher; gracious and smiling he ran up and down the aisles; nothing was too much trouble for him; he carried messages and brought programmes as though it were his greatest pleasure in life, and all the people in his section thought him a charming boy, feeling that he remembered and admired them. As the house filled, he grew more and more vivacious and animated, and the colour came to his cheeks and lips. It was very much as though this were a great reception and Paul were the host. Just as the musicians came out to take their places, his English teacher arrived with checks for the seats which a prominent manufacturer had taken for the season. She betrayed some embarrassment when she handed Paul the tickets, and a *hauteur* which subsequently made her feel very foolish. Paul was startled for a moment, and had the feeling of wanting to put her out; what business had she here among all these fine people and gay colours? He looked her over and decided that she was not appropriately dressed and must be a fool to sit downstairs in such togs. The tickets had probably been sent her out of kindness, he reflected as he put down a seat for her, and she had about as much right to sit there as he had.

When the symphony began Paul sank into one of the rear seats with a long sigh of relief, and lost himself as he had done before the Rico. It was not that symphonies, as such, meant anything in particular to Paul, but the first sigh of the instruments seemed to free some hilarious and potent spirit within him; something that struggled there like the genie in the bottle found by the Arab fisherman. He felt a sudden zest for life; the lights danced before his eyes and the concert hall blazed into unimaginable splendour. When the soprano solo-ist came on, Paul forgot even the nastiness of his teacher's being there and gave himself up to the peculiar stimulus such personages always had for him. The soloist chanced to be a German woman, by no means in her first youth, and the mother of many children; but she wore an elaborate gown and a tiara, and above all she had that indefinable air of achieve-ment, that world-shine upon her, which, in Paul's eyes, made her a veritable queen of Romance.

After a concert was over Paul was always irritable and wretched until he got to sleep, and tonight he was even more then usually restless. He had the feeling of not being able to let down, of its being impossible to give up this delicious excitement which was the only thing that could be called living at all. During the last number he withdrew and, after hastily changing his clothes in the dressing-room, slipped out to the side door where the soprano's carriage stood. Here he began pacing rapidly up and down the walk, waiting to see her come out.

Over yonder the Schenley, in its vacant stretch, loomed big and square through the fine rain, the windows of its twelve stories glowing like those of a lighted card-board house under a Christmas tree. All the actors and singers of the better class stayed there when they were in the city, and a number of the big manufacturers of the place lived there in the winter. Paul had often hung about the hotel, watching the people go in and out, longing to enter and leave school-masters and dull care behind him forever.

At last the singer came out, accompanied by the conductor, who helped her into her carriage and closed the door with a cordial *auf wiedersehen*, which set Paul to wondering whether she were not an old sweetheart of his. Paul followed the carriage over to the hotel, walking so rapidly as not to be far from the entrance when the singer alighted and disappeared behind the swinging glass doors that were opened by a negro in a tall hat and a long coat. In the moment that the door was ajar, it seemed to Paul that he, too, entered. He seemed to feel himself go after her up the steps, into the warm, lighted building, into an exotic, a tropical world of shiny, glistening surfaces and basking ease. He reflected upon the mysterious dishes that were brought into the dining-room, the green bottles in buckets of ice, as he had seen them in the supper party pictures of the *Sunday World* supplement. A quick gust of wind brought the rain down with sudden vehemence, and Paul was startled to find that he was still outside in the slush of the gravel driveway; that his boots were letting in the water and his scanty overcoat was clinging wet about him; that the lights in front of the concert hall were out, and that the rain was driving in sheets between him and the orange glow of the windows above him. There it was, what he wanted—tangibly before him, like the fairy world of a Christmas pantomime, but mocking spirits stood guard at the doors, and, as the rain beat in his face, Paul wondered whether he were destined always to shiver in the black night outside, looking up at it.

He turned and walked reluctantly toward the car tracks. The end had to come sometime; his father in his night-clothes at the top of the stairs, explanations that did not explain, hastily improvised fictions that were forever tripping him up, his upstairs room and its horrible yellow wall-paper, the creaking bureau with the greasy plush collarbox, and over his painted wooden bed the pictures of George Washington and

John Calvin, and the framed motto, "Feed my Lambs," which had been worked in red worsted by his mother.

Half an hour later, Paul alighted from his car and went slowly down one of the side streets off the main thoroughfare. It was a highly respectable street, where all the houses were exactly alike, and where business men of moderate means begot and reared large families of children, all of whom went to Sabbath-school and learned the shorter catechism, and were interested in arithmetic; all of whom were as exactly alike as their homes, and of a piece with the monotony in which they lived. Paul never went up Cordelia Street without a shudder of loathing. His home was next to the house of the Cumberland minister. He approached it tonight with the nerveless sense of defeat, the hopeless feeling of sinking back forever into ugliness and commonness that he had always had when he came home. The moment he turned into Cordelia Street he felt the waters close above his head. After each of these orgies of living, he experienced all the physical depression which follows a debauch; the loathing of respectable beds, of common food, of a house permeated by kitchen odours; a shuddering repulsion for the flavourless, colourless mass of every-day existence; a morbid desire for cool things and soft lights and fresh flowers.

The nearer he approached the house, the more absolutely unequal Paul felt to the sight of it all; his ugly sleeping cham-

SIMON VAN BOOY

ber, the cold bathroom with the grimy zinc tub, the cracked mirror, the dripping spiggots; his father, at the top of the stairs, his hairy legs sticking out from his night-shirt, his feet thrust into carpet slippers. He was so much later than usual that there would certainly be inquiries and reproaches. Paul stopped short before the door. He felt that he could not be accosted by his father tonight; that he could not toss again on that miserable bed. He would not go in. He would tell his father that he had no car fare, and it was raining so hard he had gone home with one of the boys and stayed all night.

Meanwhile, he was wet and cold. He went around to the back of the house and tried one of the basement windows, found it open, raised it cautiously, and scrambled down the cellar wall to the floor. There he stood, holding his breath, terrified by the noise he had made, but the floor above him was silent, and there was no creak on the stairs. He found a soap-box, and carried it over to the soft ring of light that streamed from the furnace door, and sat down. He was horribly afraid of rats, so he did not try to sleep, but sat looking distrustfully at the dark, still terrified lest he might have awakened his father. In such reactions, after one of the experiences which made days and nights out of the dreary blanks of the calendar, when his senses were deadened, Paul's head was always singularly clear. Suppose his father had heard him getting in at the window and had come down and shot him for a burglar?

Then, again, suppose his father had come down, pistol in hand, and he had cried out in time to save himself, and his father had been horrified to think how nearly he had killed him? Then, again, suppose a day should come when his father would remember that night, and wish there had been no warning cry to stay his hand? With this last supposition Paul entertained himself until daybreak.

The following Sunday was fine; the sodden November chill was broken by the last flash of autumnal summer. In the morning Paul had to go to church and Sabbath-school, as always. On seasonable Sunday afternoons the burghers of Cordelia Street always sat out on their front "stoops," and talked to their neighbours on the next stoop, or called to those across the street in neighbourly fashion. The men usually sat on gay cushions placed upon the steps that led down to the sidewalk, while the women, in their Sunday "waists," sat in rockers on the cramped porches, pretending to be greatly at their ease. The children played in the streets; there were so many of them that the place resembled the recreation grounds of a kindergarten. The men on the steps—all in their shirtsleeves, their vests unbuttoned—sat with their legs well apart, their stomachs comfortably protruding, and talked of the prices of things, or told anecdotes of the sagacity of their various chiefs and overlords. They occasionally looked over the multitude of squabbling children, listened affectionately to their

SIMON VAN BOOY

high-pitched, nasal voices, smiling to see their own proclivities reproduced in their offspring, and interspersed their legends of the iron kings with remarks about their sons' progress at school, their grades in arithmetic, and the amounts they had saved in their toy banks.

On this last Sunday of November, Paul sat all the afternoon on the lowest step of his "stoop," staring into the street, while his sisters, in their rockers, were talking to the minister's daughters next door about how many shirt-waists they had made in the last week, and how many waffles some one had eaten at the last church supper. When the weather was warm, and his father was in a particularly jovial frame of mind, the girls made lemonade, which was always brought out in a red-glass pitcher, ornamented with forget-me-nots in blue enamel. This the girls thought very fine, and the neighbours always joked about the suspicious colour of the pitcher.

Today Paul's father sat on the top step, talking to a young man who shifted a restless baby from knee to knee. He happened to be the young man who was daily held up to Paul as a model, and after whom it was his father's dearest hope that he would pattern. This young man was of a ruddy complexion, with a compressed, red mouth, and faded, near-sighted eyes, over which he wore thick spectacles, with gold bows that curved about his ears. He was clerk to one of the magnates of a great steel corporation, and was looked upon in Cordelia

Street as a young man with a future. There was a story that, some five years ago—he was now barely twenty-six—he had been a trifle dissipated, but in order to curb his appetites and save the loss of time and strength that a sowing of wild oats might have entailed, he had taken his chief's advice, oft reiterated to his employees, and at twenty-one had married the first woman whom he could persuade to share his fortunes. She happened to be an angular school-mistress, much older than he, who also wore thick glasses, and who had now borne him four children, all near-sighted, like herself.

The young man was relating how his chief, now cruising in the Mediterranean, kept in touch with all the details of the business, arranging his office hours on his yacht just as though he were at home, and "knocking off work enough to keep two stenographers busy." His father told, in turn, the plan his corporation was considering, of putting in an electric railway plant at Cairo. Paul snapped his teeth; he had an awful apprehension that they might spoil it all before he got there. Yet he rather liked to hear these legends of the iron kings, that were told and retold on Sundays and holidays; these stories of palaces in Venice, yachts on the Mediterranean, and high play at Monte Carlo appealed to his fancy, and he was interested in the triumphs of these cash boys who had become famous, though he had no mind for the cash-boy stage.

After supper was over, and he had helped to dry the dishes, Paul nervously asked his father whether he could go to George's to get some help in his geometry, and still more nervously asked for car fare. This latter request he had to repeat, as his father, on principle, did not like to hear requests for money, whether much or little. He asked Paul whether he could not go to some boy who lived nearer, and told him that he ought not to leave his school work until Sunday; but he gave him the dime. He was not a poor man, but he had a worthy ambition to come up in the world. His only reason for allowing Paul to usher was, that he thought a boy ought to be earning a little.

Paul bounded upstairs, scrubbed the greasy odour of the dish-water from his hands with the ill-smelling soap he hated, and then shook over his fingers a few drops of violet water from the bottle he kept hidden in his drawer. He left the house with his geometry conspicuously under his arm, and the moment he got out of Cordelia Street and boarded a downtown car, he shook off the lethargy of two deadening days, and began to live again.

The leading juvenile of the permanent stock company which played at one of the downtown theatres was an acquaintance of Paul's, and the boy had been invited to drop in at the Sunday-night rehearsals whenever he could. For more than a year Paul had spent every available moment loitering about Charley Edwards's dressing-room. He had won a place among Edwards's following not only because the young actor, who could not afford to employ a dresser, often found him useful, but because he recognized in Paul something akin to what churchmen term "vocation."

It was at the theatre and at Carnegie Hall that Paul really lived; the rest was but a sleep and a forgetting. This was Paul's fairy tale, and it had for him all the allurement of a secret love. The moment he inhaled the gassy, painty, dusty odour behind the scenes, he breathed like a prisoner set free, and felt within him the possibility of doing or saying splendid, brilliant, poetic things. The moment the cracked orchestra beat out the over-ture from *Martha*, or jerked at the serenade from *Rigoletto*, all stupid and ugly things slid from him, and his senses were deliciously, yet delicately fired.

Perhaps it was because, in Paul's world, the natural nearly always wore the guise of ugliness, that a certain element of ar-tificiality seemed to him necessary in beauty. Perhaps it was because his experience of life elsewhere was so full of Sabbath-school picnics, petty economies, wholesome advice as to how to succeed in life, and the unescapable odours of cooking, that he found this existence so alluring, these smartly-clad men and women so attractive, that he was so moved by these starry apple orchards that bloomed perennially under the limelight.

It would be difficult to put it strongly enough how con-vincingly the stage entrance of that theatre was for Paul the actual portal of Romance. Certainly none of the company ever suspected it, least of all Charley Edwards. It was very like the old stories that used to float about London of fabulously rich Jews, who had subterranean halls there, with palms, and fountains, and soft lamps and richly apparelled women who never saw the disenchanting light of London day. So, in the midst of that smoke-palled city, enamoured of figures and grimy toil, Paul had his secret temple, his wishing carpet, his bit of blue-and-white Mediterranean shore bathed in perpetual sunshine.

Several of Paul's teachers had a theory that his imagination had been perverted by garish fiction, but the truth was that he scarcely ever read at all. The books at home were not such as would either tempt or corrupt a youthful mind, and as for reading the novels that some of his friends urged upon him—well, he got what he wanted much more quickly from music; any sort of music, from an orchestra to a barrel organ. He needed only the spark, the indescribable thrill that made his imagination master of his senses, and he could make plots and pictures enough of his own. It was equally true that he was not stage-struck—not, at any rate, in the usual acceptation of that expression. He had no desire to become an actor, any more than he had to become a musician. He felt no necessity to do any of these things; what he wanted was to see, to be in the atmosphere, float on the wave of it, to be carried out, blue league after blue league, away from everything.

After a night behind the scenes, Paul found the schoolroom more than ever repulsive; the bare floors and naked walls; the prosy men who never wore frock coats, or violets in their buttonholes; the women with their dull gowns, shrill voices, and pitiful seriousness about prepositions that govern the dative. He could not bear to have the other pupils think, for a moment, that he took these people seriously; he must convey to them that he considered it all trivial, and was there only by way of a jest, anyway. He had autograph pictures of all the members of the stock company which he showed his classmates, telling them the most incredible stories of his familiarity with these people, of his acquaintance with the soloists who came to Carnegie Hall, his suppers with them and the flowers he sent them. When these stories lost their effect, and his audience grew listless, he became desperate and would bid all the boys good-bye, announcing that he was going to travel for awhile; going to Naples, to Venice, to Egypt. Then, next Monday, he would slip back, conscious and nervously smiling; his sister was ill, and he should have to defer his voyage until spring.

Matters went steadily worse with Paul at school. In the itch to let his instructors know how heartily he despised them and their homilies, and how thoroughly he was appreciated elsewhere, he mentioned once or twice that he had no time to fool with theorems; adding—with a twitch of the eyebrows and a touch of that nervous bravado which so perplexed them—

that he was helping the people down at the stock company; they were old friends of his.

The upshot of the matter was, that the Principal went to Paul's father, and Paul was taken out of school and put to work. The manager at Carnegie Hall was told to get another usher in his stead; the doorkeeper at the theatre was warned not to admit him to the house; and Charley Edwards remorsefully promised the boy's father not to see him again.

The members of the stock company were vastly amused when some of Paul's stories reached them—especially the women. They were hardworking women, most of them supporting indigent husbands or brothers, and they laughed rather bitterly at having stirred the boy to such fervid and florid inventions. They agreed with the faculty and with his father that Paul's was a bad case.

The east-bound train was ploughing through a January snowstorm; the dull dawn was beginning to show grey when the engine whistled a mile out of Newark. Paul started up from the seat where he had lain curled in uneasy slumber, rubbed the breath-misted window glass with his hand, and peered out. The snow was whirling in curling eddies above the white bottom lands, and the drifts lay already deep in the fields and along the fences, while here and there the long dead grass and dried weed stalks protruded black above it. Lights shone from the scattered houses, and a gang of labourers who stood beside the track waved their lanterns.

Paul had slept very little, and he felt grimy and uncomfortable. He had made the all-night journey in a day coach, partly because he was ashamed, dressed as he was, to go into a Pullman, and partly because he was afraid of being seen there by some Pittsburgh business man, who might have noticed him in Denny & Carson's office. When the whistle awoke him, he clutched quickly at his breast pocket, glancing about him with an uncertain smile. But the little, clay-bespattered Italians were still sleeping, the slatternly women across the aisle were in open-mouthed oblivion, and even the crumby, crying babies were for the nonce stilled. Paul settled back to struggle with his impatience as best he could.

When he arrived at the Jersey City station, he hurried through his breakfast, manifestly ill at ease and keeping a sharp eye about him. After he reached the Twenty-third Street station, he consulted a cabman, and had himself driven to a men's furnishing establishment that was just opening for the day. He spent upward of two hours there, buying with endless reconsidering and great care. His new street suit he put on in the fitting-room; the frock coat and dress clothes he had bundled into the cab with his linen. Then he drove to a hatter's and a shoe house. His next errand was at Tiffany's, where he selected his silver and a new scarf-pin. He would not wait to have his silver marked, he said. Lastly, he stopped at a trunk shop on Broadway, and had his purchases packed into various traveling bags.

It was a little after one o'clock when he drove up to the Waldorf, and after settling with the cabman, went into the office. He registered from Washington; said his mother and father had been abroad, and that he had come down to await the arrival of their steamer. He told his story plausibly and had no trouble, since he volunteered to pay for them in advance, in engaging his rooms; a sleeping-room, sitting-room and bath.

Not once, but a hundred times Paul had planned this entry into New York. He had gone over every detail of it with Charley Edwards, and in his scrap book at home there were pages of description about New York hotels, cut from the Sunday papers. When he was shown to his sitting-room on the eighth floor, he saw at a glance that everything was as it should be; there was but one detail in his mental picture that the place did not realize, so he rang for the bell boy and sent him down for flowers. He moved about nervously until the boy returned, putting away his new linen and fingering it delightedly as he did so. When the flowers came, he put them hastily into water, and then tumbled into a hot bath. Presently he came out of his white bathroom, resplendent in his new silk underwear, and playing with the tassels of his red robe. The snow was whirling so fiercely outside his windows that he could scarcely see across the street, but within the air was deliciously soft and fragrant. He put the violets and jonquils on the taboret beside the couch, and threw himself down, with a long sigh, covering himself with a Roman blanket. He was thoroughly tired; he had been in such haste, he had stood up to such a strain, covered so much ground in the last twenty-four hours, that he wanted to think how it had all come about. Lulled by the sound of the wind, the warm air, and the cool fragrance of the flowers, he sank into deep, drowsy retrospection.

It had been wonderfully simple; when they had shut him out of the theatre and concert hall, when they had taken away his bone, the whole thing was virtually determined. The rest was a mere matter of opportunity. The only thing that at all surprised him was his own courage—for he realized well enough that he had always been tormented by fear, a sort of apprehensive dread that, of late years, as the meshes of the lies he had told closed about him, had been pulling the muscles of his body tighter and tighter. Until now, he could not remember the time when he had not been dreading something. Even when he was a little boy, it was always there—behind him, or before, or on either side. There had always been the shadowed corner, the dark place into which he dared not look, but from which something seemed always to be watching him—and Paul had done things that were not pretty to watch, he knew.

But now he had a curious sense of relief, as though he had at last thrown down the gauntlet to the thing in the corner.

Yet it was but a day since he had been sulking in the traces; but yesterday afternoon that he had been sent to the bank with Denny & Carson's deposit, as usual—but this time he was instructed to leave the book to be balanced. There was above two thousand dollars in checks, and nearly a thousand in the bank notes which he had taken from the book and quietly transferred to his pocket. At the bank he had made out a new deposit slip. His nerves had been steady enough to permit of his returning to the office, where he had finished his work and asked for a full day's holiday tomorrow, Saturday, giving a perfectly reasonable pretext. The bank book, he knew, would not be returned before Monday or Tuesday, and his father would be out of town for the next week. From the time he slipped the bank notes into his pocket until he boarded the night train for New York, he had not known a moment's hesitation. It was not the first time Paul had steered through treacherous waters.

How astonishingly easy it had all been; here he was, the thing done; and this time there would be no awakening, no figure at the top of the stairs. He watched the snow flakes whirling by his window until he fell asleep.

When he awoke, it was three o'clock in the afternoon. He bounded up with a start; half of one of his precious days gone already! He spent more than an hour in dressing, watching every stage of his toilet carefully in the mirror. Everything was quite perfect; he was exactly the kind of boy he had always wanted to be.

When he went downstairs, Paul took a carriage and drove up Fifth Avenue toward the Park. The snow had somewhat abated; carriages and tradesmen's wagons were hurrying soundlessly to and fro in the winter twilight; boys in woolen mufflers were shovelling off the doorsteps; the avenue stages made fine spots of colour against the white street. Here and there on the corners were stands, with whole flower gardens blooming under glass cases, against the sides of which the snow flakes stuck and melted; violets, roses, carnations, lilies of the valley—somehow vastly more lovely and alluring that they blossomed thus unnaturally in the snow. The Park itself was a wonderful stage winter-piece.

When he returned, the pause of the twilight had ceased, and the tune of the streets had changed. The snow was falling faster, lights streamed from the hotels that reared their dozen stories fearlessly up into the storm, defying the raging Atlantic winds. A long, black stream of carriages poured down the avenue, intersected here and there by other streams, tending horizontally. There were a score of cabs about the entrance of his hotel, and the driver had to wait. Boys in livery were running in and out of the awning stretched across the sidewalk, up and down the red velvet carpet laid from the door to the street. Above, about, within it all was the rumble and roar, the hurry and toss of thousands of human beings as hot for pleasure as himself, and on every side of him towered the glaring affirmation of the omnipotence of wealth.

The boy set his teeth and drew his shoulders together in a spasm of realization; the plot of all dramas, the text of all romances, the nerve-stuff of all sensations was whirling about him like the snow flakes. He burnt like a faggot in a tempest.

When Paul went down to dinner, the music of the orchestra came floating up the elevator shaft to greet him. His head whirled as he stepped into the thronged corridor, and he sank back into one of the chairs against the wall to get his breath. The lights, the chatter, the perfumes, the bewildering medley of colour—he had, for a moment, the feeling of not being able to stand it. But only for a moment; these were his own people, he told himself. He went slowly about the corridors, through the writing-rooms, smoking-rooms, reception-rooms, as though he were exploring the chambers of an enchanted palace, built and peopled for him alone.

When he reached the dining-room he sat down at a table near a window. The flowers, the white linen, the many-coloured wine glasses, the gay toilettes of the women, the low popping of corks, the undulating repetitions of the *Blue Danube* from the orchestra, all flooded Paul's dream with bewildering radiance. When the roseate tinge of his champagne was added—that cold, precious bubbling stuff that creamed and foamed in his glass—Paul wondered that there were honest men in the world at all. This was what all the world was fighting for, he reflected; this was what all the struggle was about. He doubted the reality of his past. Had he ever known a place called Cordelia Street, a place where fagged-looking business men got on the early car; mere rivets in a machine they seemed to Paul—sickening men, with combings of children's hair always hanging to their coats, and the smell of cooking in their clothes. Cordelia Street—Ah! that belonged to another time and country; had he not always been thus, had he not sat here night after night, from as far back as he could remember, looking pensively over just such shimmering textures, and slowly twirling the stem of a glass like this one between his thumb and middle finger? He rather thought he had.

He was not in the least abashed or lonely. He had no especial desire to meet or to know any of these people; all he demanded was the right to look on and conjecture, to watch the pageant. The mere stage properties were all he contended for. Nor was he lonely later in the evening, in his loge at the Metropolitan. He was now entirely rid of his nervous misgivings, of his forced aggressiveness, of the imperative desire to show himself different from his surroundings. He felt now that his

SIMON VAN BOOY

surroundings explained him. Nobody questioned the purple; he had only to wear it passively. He had only to glance down at his attire to reassure himself that here it would be impossible for any one to humiliate him.

He found it hard to leave his beautiful sitting-room to go to bed that night, and sat long watching the raging storm from his turret window. When he went to sleep, it was with the lights turned on in his bedroom; partly because of his old timidity, and partly so that, if he should wake in the night, there would be no wretched moment of doubt, no horrible suspicion of yellow wall-paper, or of Washington and Calvin above his bed.

Sunday morning the city was practically snow-bound. Paul breakfasted late, and in the afternoon he fell in with a wild San Francisco boy, a freshman at Yale, who said he had run down for a "little flyer" over Sunday. The young man offered to show Paul the night side of the town, and the two boys went out together after dinner, not returning to the hotel until seven o'clock the next morning. They had started out in the confiding warmth of a champagne friendship, but their parting in the elevator was singularly cool. The freshman pulled himself together to make his train, and Paul went to bed. He awoke at two o'clock in the afternoon, very thirsty and dizzy, and rang for ice-water, coffee, and the Pittsburgh papers.

On the part of the hotel management, Paul excited no suspicion. There was this to be said for him, that he wore his spoils with dignity and in no way made himself conspicuous. Even under the glow of his wine he was never boisterous, though he found the stuff like a magician's wand for wonder-building. His chief greediness lay in his ears and eyes, and his excesses were not offensive ones. His dearest pleasures were the grey winter twilights in his sitting-room; his quiet enjoyment of his flowers, his clothes, his wide divan, his cigarette and his sense of power. He could not remember a time when he had felt so at peace with himself. The mere release from the necessity of petty lying, lying every day and every day, restored his self-respect. He had never lied for pleasure, even at school; but to be noticed and admired, to assert his difference from other Cordelia Street boys; and he felt a good deal more manly, more honest, even, now that he had no need for boastful pretensions, now that he could, as his actor friends used to say, "dress the part." It was characteristic that remorse did not occur to him. His golden days went by without a shadow, and he made each as perfect as he could.

On the eighth day after his arrival in New York, he found the whole affair exploited in the Pittsburgh papers, exploited with a wealth of detail which indicated that local news of a sensational nature was at a low ebb. The firm of Denny & Carson announced that the boy's father had refunded the full amount of the theft, and that they had no intention of prosecuting. The Cumberland minister had been interviewed, and

SIMON VAN BOOY

expressed his hope of yet reclaiming the motherless lad, and his Sabbath-school teacher declared that she would spare no effort to that end. The rumour had reached Pittsburgh that the boy had been seen in a New York hotel, and his father had gone East to find him and bring him home.

Paul had just come in to dress for dinner; he sank into a chair, weak to the knees, and clasped his head in his hands. It was to be worse than jail, even; the tepid waters of Cordelia Street were to close over him finally and forever. The grey monotony stretched before him in hopeless, unrelieved years; Sabbath-school, Young People's Meeting, the yellow-papered room, the damp dish-towels; it all rushed back upon him with a sickening vividness. He had the old feeling that the orchestra had suddenly stopped, the sinking sensation that the play was over. The sweat broke out on his face, and he sprang to his feet, looked about him with his white, conscious smile, and winked at himself in the mirror. With something of the old childish belief in miracles with which he had so often gone to class, all his lessons unlearned, Paul dressed and dashed whistling down the corridor to the elevator.

He had no sooner entered the dining-room and caught the measure of the music than his remembrance was lightened by his old elastic power of claiming the moment, mounting with it, and finding it all sufficient. The glare and glitter about him, the mere scenic accessories had again, and for the last time, their old potency. He would show himself that he was game, he would finish the thing splendidly. He doubted, more than ever, the existence of Cordelia Street, and for the first time he drank his wine recklessly. Was he not, after all, one of those fortunate beings born to the purple, was he not still himself and in his own place? He drummed a nervous accompaniment to the Pagliacci music and looked about him, telling himself over and over that it had paid.

He reflected drowsily, to the swell of the music and the chill sweetness of his wine, that he might have done it more wisely. He might have caught an outbound steamer and been well out of their clutches before now. But the other side of the world had seemed too far away and too uncertain then; he could not have waited for it; his need had been too sharp. If he had to choose over again, he would do the same thing tomorrow. He looked affectionately about the dining-room, now gilded with a soft mist. Ah, it had paid indeed!

Paul was awakened next morning by a painful throbbing in his head and feet. He had thrown himself across the bed without undressing, and had slept with his shoes on. His limbs and hands were lead heavy, and his tongue and throat were parched and burnt. There came upon him one of those fateful attacks of clear-headedness that never occurred except when he was physically exhausted and his nerves hung loose. He lay still and closed his eyes and let the tide of things wash over him.

His father was in New York; "stopping at some joint or other," he told himself. The memory of successive summers on the front stoop fell upon him like a weight of black water. He had not a hundred dollars left; and he knew now, more than ever, that money was everything, the wall that stood between all he loathed and all he wanted. The thing was winding itself up; he had thought of that on his first glorious day in New York, and had even provided a way to snap the thread. It lay on his dressing-table now; he had got it out last night when he came blindly up from dinner, but the shiny metal hurt his eyes, and he disliked the looks of it.

He rose and moved about with a painful effort, succumbing now and again to attacks of nausea. It was the old depression exaggerated; all the world had become Cordelia Street. Yet somehow he was not afraid of anything, was absolutely calm; perhaps because he had looked into the dark corner at last and knew. It was bad enough, what he saw there, but somehow not so bad as his long fear of it had been. He saw everything clearly now. He had a feeling that he had made the best of it, that he had lived the sort of life he was meant to live, and for half an hour he sat staring at the revolver. But he told himself that was not the way, so he went downstairs and took a cab to the ferry.

When Paul arrived at Newark, he got off the train and took another cab, directing the driver to follow the Pennsylvania tracks out of the town. The snow lay heavy on the roadways and had drifted deep in the open fields. Only here and there the dead grass or dried weed stalks projected, singularly black, above it. Once well into the country, Paul dismissed the carriage and walked, floundering along the tracks, his mind a medley of irrelevant things. He seemed to hold in his brain an actual picture of everything he had seen that morning. He remembered every feature of both his drivers, of the toothless old woman from whom he had bought the red flowers in his coat, the agent from whom he had got his ticket, and all of his fellow-passengers on the ferry. His mind, unable to cope with vital matters near at hand, worked feverishly and deftly at sorting and grouping these images. They made for him a part of the ugliness of the world, of the ache in his head, and the bitter burning on his tongue. He stopped and put a handful of snow into his mouth as he walked, but that, too, seemed hot. When he reached a little hillside, where the tracks ran through a cut some twenty feet below him, he stopped and sat down.

The carnations in his coat were drooping with the cold, he noticed; their red glory all over. It occurred to him that all the flowers he had seen in the glass cases that first night must have gone the same way, long before this. It was only one splendid breath they had, in spite of their brave mockery at the winter outside the glass; and it was a losing game in the end, it seemed, this revolt against the homilies by which the world is run. Paul took one of the blossoms carefully from his coat and scooped a little hole in the snow, where he covered it up. Then he dozed a while, from his weak condition, seeming insensible to the cold.

The sound of an approaching train awoke him, and he started to his feet, remembering only his resolution, and afraid lest he should be too late. He stood watching the approaching locomotive, his teeth chattering, his lips drawn away from them in a frightened smile; once or twice he glanced nervously sidewise, as though he were being watched. When the right moment came, he jumped. As he fell, the folly of his haste occurred to him with merciless clearness, the vastness of what he had left undone. There flashed through his brain, clearer than ever before, the blue of Adriatic water, the yellow of Algerian sands.

Thich Nhat Hanh is a Buddhist Zen master, poet, and human rights activist. Born in 1926, he has devoted his life to helping individuals with their basic needs for survival and to find a sense of deep fulfillment through self-reflection, mindfulness, compassion, and nonviolence. Nhat Hanh publicly requested Dr. Martin Luther King Jr. to oppose the Vietnam War and was nominated for the Nobel Peace Prize one year later. In 1982, he founded Plum Village, a Buddhist community in France, where he continues his human rights advocacy and runs retreat programs.

In his book, *True Love*, Nhat Hanh explores the idea that to love, one must be present.

Thich Nhat Hanh

"Love Is Being There" from *True Love*

To love, in the context of Buddhism, is above all to be there. But being there is not an easy thing. Some training is necessary, some practice. If you are not there, how can you love? Being there is very much an art, the art of meditation, because meditating is bringing your true presence to the here and now. The question that arises is: Do you have time to love?

I know a boy of twelve whose father asked him one day:

"Son, what would you like for your birthday present?" The boy did not know how to answer his father, who was a very rich man, able to buy anything for his son. But the boy did not want anything except his father's presence. Because the role the father played kept him very busy, he did not have time to devote to his wife and children. Being rich is an obstacle to loving. When you are rich, you want to continue to be rich, and so you end up devoting all your time, all your energy in your daily life, to staying rich. If this father were to understand what true love is, he would do whatever is necessary to find time for his son and his wife.

The most precious gift you can give to the one you love is your true presence. What must we do to really be there? Those who have practiced Buddhist meditation know that meditating is above all being present: to yourself, to those you love, to life.

So I would propose a very simple practice to you, the practice of mindful breathing: "Breathing—I know that I am breathing in; breathing—I know that I am breathing out." If you do that with a little concentration, then you will be able to really be there, because in our daily life our mind and our body are rarely together. Our body might be there, but our mind is somewhere else. Maybe you are lost in regrets about the past, maybe in worries about the future, or else you are preoccupied with your plans, with anger or with jealousy. And so your mind is not really there with your body.

Between the mind and the body, there is something that can serve as a bridge. The moment you begin to practice mindful breathing, your body and your mind begin to come together with one another. It takes only ten to twenty seconds to accomplish this miracle called oneness of body and mind. With mindful breathing, you can bring body and mind together in the present moment, and every one of us can do it, even a child.

The Buddha left us an absolutely essential text, the *Anapanasati Sutta*, or *Discourse on the Practice of Mindful Breathing*. If you really want to practice Buddhist meditation, you must study this text.

If the father I was talking about had known that, he would have begun to breathe in and breathe out mindfully, and then one or two minutes later, he would have approached his son, he would have looked at him with a smile, and he would have said this: "My dear, I am here for you." This is the greatest gift you can give to someone you love.

In Buddhism we talk about mantras. A mantra is a magic formula that, once it is uttered, can entirely change a situation, our mind, our body, or a person. But this magic formula must be spoken in a state of concentration, that is to say, a state in which body and mind are absolutely in a state of unity. What you say then, in this state of being, becomes a mantra.

So I am going to present to you a very effective mantra, not in Sanskrit or Tibetan, but in English: "Dear one, I am here for you." Perhaps this evening you will try for a few minutes to practice mindful breathing in order to bring your body and mind together. You will approach the person you love and with this mindfulness, with this concentration, you will look into his or her eyes, and you will begin to utter this formula: "Dear one, I am really here for you." You must say that with your body and with your mind at the same time, and then you will see the transformation.

Do you have enough time to love? Can you make sure that in your everyday life you have a little time to love? We do not have much time together; we are too busy. In the morning while eating breakfast, we do not look at the person we love, we do not have enough time for it. We eat very quickly while thinking about other things, and sometimes we even hold a newspaper that hides the face of the person we love. In the evening when we come home, we are too tired to be able to look at the person we love.

We must bring about a revolution in our way of living our everyday lives, because our happiness, our lives, are within ourselves.

Born into a Roman Catholic family in 1572, John Donne's father died when he was four years old. As a young man, Donne spent his inheritance on books, theater, travel, and women. However, in 1601, aged twenty-nine, he married the seventeen-year-old daughter of a high-ranking official, who had his new son-in-law fired and then sent to prison for a few weeks. Although after eight years Donne and his father-in-law were reconciled, Donne's wife died, in 1617, after giving birth to a stillborn child. Donne was left a single father of seven. By 1621, Donne was one of the most influential men in England. He died ten years later in 1631.

John Donne

"The Legacy"

When I died last, and, dear, I die
   As often as from thee I go,
   Though it be but an hour ago,
And lovers' hours be full eternity,
I can remember yet, that I
   Something did say, and something did bestow;
Though I be dead, which sent me, I should be
Mine own executor and legacy.

I heard me say: "Tell her anon,
   That my self, (that is you, not I,)
   Did kill me," and when I felt me die,
I bid me send my heart, when I was gone;
But I alas could there find none,
   When I had ripped me, and searched where hearts did lie;
It killed me again, that I who still was true,
In life, in my last will should cozen you.

Yet I found something like a heart,
   But colours it, and corners had,
   It was not good, it was not bad,
It was entire to none, and few had part.

As good as could be made by art

    It seemed; and therefore for our losses sad,

I meant to send this heart instead of mine,

But oh, no man could hold it, for 'twas thine.

John Donne

"The Dream"

Dear love, for nothing less than thee
Would I have broke this happy dream,
     It was a theme
For reason, much too strong for phantasy,
Therefore thou waked'st me wisely; yet
My dream thou brokest not, but continued'st it;
Thou art so truth, that thoughts of thee suffice,
To make dreams truths, and fables histories;
Enter these arms, for since thou thought'st it best,
Not to dream all my dream, let's act the rest.

As lightning, or a taper's light,
Thine eyes, and not thy noise waked me;
     Yet I thought thee
(For thou lovest truth) an angel, at first sight,
But when I saw thou sawest my heart,
And knew'st my thoughts, beyond an angel's art,
When thou knew'st what I dreamt, when thou knew'st when
Excess of joy would wake me, and cam'st then,
I must confess, it could not choose but be
Profane, to think thee anything but thee.

Coming and staying showed thee, thee,
But rising makes me doubt, that now,
   Thou art not thou.
That love is weak, where fear's as strong as he;
'Tis not all spirit, pure, and brave,
If mixture it of *Fear, Shame, Honour*, have.
Perchance as torches which must ready be,
Men light and put out, so thou deal'st with me,
Thou cam'st to kindle, goest to come; then I
Will dream that hope again, but else would die.

William Shakespeare was born in 1564 in the reign of Queen Elizabeth I. He grew up in Stratford-upon-Avon in central England, one of eight children. Although he probably attended school, he did not go to university. When he was eighteen, he married Anne Hathaway, a woman eight years his senior, who gave birth to their first child about six months after the marriage ceremony. Shakespeare lived most of his adult life in London, where he worked as an actor and playwright with the successful Lord Chamberlain's Men. He died in 1616. His plays have since been translated into every major living language.

William Shakespeare

Scene II from *The Tragedy of Romeo and Juliet*

ROMEO

JULIET (APPEARS ABOVE AT A WINDOW)

But, soft! what light through yonder window breaks?

It is the east, and Juliet is the sun.

Arise, fair sun, and kill the envious moon,

Who is already sick and pale with grief,

That thou her maid art far more fair than she:

Be not her maid, since she is envious;

Her vestal livery is but sick and green

And none but fools do wear it; cast it off.

It is my lady, O, it is my love!

O, that she knew she were!

She speaks yet she says nothing: what of that?

Her eye discourses; I will answer it.

I am too bold, 'tis not to me she speaks:

Two of the fairest stars in all the heaven,

Having some business, do entreat her eyes

To twinkle in their spheres till they return.

What if her eyes were there, they in her head?

The brightness of her cheek would shame those stars,

As daylight doth a lamp; her eyes in heaven

Would through the airy region stream so bright
That birds would sing and think it were not night.
See, how she leans her cheek upon her hand!
O, that I were a glove upon that hand,
That I might touch that cheek!

. . . Theo, I love her, her and no other, her forever. And, and, and, Theo, although the "no, never, ever" still "seems" to be in full sway, there is a feeling of something like redemption within me, and it is as if she and I had stopped being two and were united for all eternity.

—*Vincent Van Gogh from a letter to his brother, Theo*

Edward Estlin Cummings was born in Cambridge, Massachusetts, and educated at Harvard.

After college, Cummings served as a volunteer ambulance driver in World War I in Paris, where he was imprisoned by the French authorities for more than three months on the suspicion of espionage and antiwar sentiments. After the war, Cummings returned home, living between rural Connecticut and New York City. Between 1923 and his death in 1962, Cummings wrote over a dozen books. He is perhaps most well-known for abandoning the traditional forms of poetry in favor of more experimental techniques, which came to characterize his style.

E. E. Cummings

"somewhere i have never travelled,gladly beyond"

somewhere i have never travelled,gladly beyond
any experience,your eyes have their silence:
in your most frail gesture are things which enclose me,
or which i cannot touch because they are too near

your slightest look easily will unclose me
though i have closed myself as fingers,
you open always petal by petal myself as Spring opens
(touching skilfully,mysteriously)her first rose

or if your wish be to close me, i and
my life will shut very beautifully ,suddenly,
as when the heart of this flower imagines
the snow carefully everywhere descending;

nothing which we are to perceive in this world equals
the power of your intense fragility:whose texture
compels me with the color of its countries,
rendering death and forever with each breathing

(i do not know what it is about you that closes
and opens;only something in me understands
the voice of your eyes is deeper than all roses)
nobody,not even the rain,has such small hands

Marc Chagall, *Birthday*, 1915

The next piece is a fragment taken from a poem by the Sixth Dalai Lama, who lived in the late seventeenth century. His name was Tsangyang Gyatso, and his childhood experience was one of poverty and abuse, which arose from ongoing tests designed to prove his identity as the reincarnation of the previous Dalai Lama.

Gyatso later refused to take the religious vows expected of a Dalai Lama, and was known for his eccentric outfits, his public intoxication, and his frequent visits to brothels.

Tsangyang Gyatso died when he was only twenty-three years old and left behind some interesting poetry. In this extract, human desire is framed by the gentle rhythms of nature.

Tsangyang Gyatso

From *Love Poems of the Sixth Dalai Lama*

I sought my love at twilight
Snow fell at daybreak.
Secret or not, no matter.
Footprints have been left in the snow.

Geoffrey Chaucer was an English poet, diplomat, and courtier born around 1343. Hed was schooled until he went to work as a page in the house of a duchess in his early teens. Although he was a servant, his job was an enviable one for the times, and included carrying candles, making beds, and general house duties. When he was nineteen, he went to war in France and was taken prisoner. A year later, he was offered for ransom, and powerful friends in England thought him worth freeing. Scholars speculate that Chaucer began writing poetry after he departed France for England. By 1367, Chaucer was in the king's service as a valet. About that time he married a young woman who was herself employed by the queen's requests. As Chaucer advanced in age, so did his position in society, and by 1386 he was Knight of the Shire. It was about this time Chaucer began composing *The Canterbury Tales*. He died in 1400.

Chaucer wrote *The Canterbury Tales* in Middle English—a language spoken by the common person. The unfinished manuscript brings together twenty-three stories, told by men and women on a walking pilgrimage to the tomb of St. Thomas Beckett. *The Canterbury Tales* depicts people of the 1300s as they really were—not as they were supposed to be in the eyes of the church.

The order in which the pilgrims are supposed to tell their tales reflects their station in society. However, after the Knight tells his tale—a highbrow story of classical (Greco-Roman) love, the Miller (who is exceedingly drunk), interrupts the proceedings and insists on telling his tale next, which he believes is a far more realistic portrayal of love than the Knight's Tale. From the Miller's point of view, our need for love is nothing more than pure lust.

Geoffrey Chaucer

from *The Canterbury Tales*

THE MILLER'S PROLOGUE

The Words between the Host and the Miller
Now when the knight had thus his story told,
In all the rout there was nor young nor old
But said it was a noble story, well
Worthy to be kept in mind to tell;
And specially the gentle folk, each one.
Our host, he laughed and swore, "So may I run,
But this goes well; unbuckled is the mail;
Let's see now who can tell another tale:
For certainly the game is well begun.
Now shall you tell, sir monk, if it can be done,
Something with which to pay for the knight's tale."
The miller, who with drinking was all pale,
So that unsteadily on his horse he sat,
He would not take off either hood or hat,
Nor wait for any man, in courtesy,
But all in Pilate's voice began to cry,
And by the Arms and Blood and Bones he swore,
"I have a noble story in my store,
With which I will requite the good knight's tale."

Our host saw, then, that he was drunk with ale,

And said to him: "Wait, Robin, my dear brother,

Some better man shall tell us first another:

Submit and let us work on profitably."

"Now by God's soul," cried he, "that will not I!

For I will speak, or else I'll go my way."

Our host replied: "Tell on, then, till doomsday!

You are a fool, your wit is overcome."

"Now hear me," said the miller, "all and some!

But first I make a protestation round

That I'm quite drunk, I know it by my sound:

And therefore, if I slander or mis-say,

Blame it on ale of Southwark, so I pray;

For I will tell a legend and a life

Both of a carpenter and of his wife,

And how a scholar set the good wright's cap."

The reeve replied and said: "Oh, shut your trap,

Let be your ignorant drunken ribaldry!

It is a sin, and further, great folly

To asperse any man, or him defame,

And, too, to bring upon a man's wife shame.

There are enough of other things to say."

This drunken miller spoke on in his way,

And said: "Oh, but my dear brother Oswald,

The man who has no wife is no cuckold.

But I say not, thereby, that you are one:
Many good wives there are, as women run,
And ever a thousand good to one that's bad,
As well you know yourself, unless you're mad.
Why are you angry with my story's cue?
I have a wife, begad, as well as you,
Yet I'd not, for the oxen of my plow,
Take on my shoulders more than is enow,
By judging of myself that I am one;
I will believe full well that I am none.
A husband must not be inquisitive
Of God, nor of his wife, while she's alive.
So long as he may find God's plenty there,
For all the rest he need not greatly care."
What should I say, except this miller rare
He would forgo his talk for no man there,
But told his churlish tale in his own way:
I think I'll here re-tell it, if I may.
And therefore, every gentle soul, I pray
That for God's love you'll hold not what I say
Evilly meant, but that I must rehearse,
All of their tales, the better and the worse,
Or else prove false to some of my design.
Therefore, who likes not this, let him, in fine,
Turn over page and choose another tale:

SIMON VAN BOOY

For he shall find enough, both great and small,
Of stories touching on gentility,
And holiness, and on morality;
And blame not me if you do choose amiss.
The miller was a churl, you well know this;
So was the reeve, and many another more,
And ribaldry they told from plenteous store.
Be then advised, and hold me free from blame;
Men should not be too serious at a game.

THE MILLER'S TALE

Once on a time was dwelling in Oxford
A wealthy lout who took in guests to board,
And of his craft he was a carpenter.
A poor scholar was lodging with him there,
Who'd learned the arts, but all his phantasy
Was turned to study of astrology;
And knew a certain set of theorems
And could find out by various stratagems,
If men but asked of him in certain hours
When they should have a drought or else have showers,
Or if men asked of him what should befall
To anything- I cannot reckon them all.
This clerk was called the clever Nicholas;

Of secret loves he knew and their solace;
And he kept counsel, too, for he was sly
And meek as any maiden passing by.
He had a chamber in that hostelry,
And lived alone there, without company,
All garnished with sweet herbs of good repute;
And he himself sweet-smelling as the root
Of licorice, valerian, or setwall.
His Almagest, and books both great and small,
His astrolabe, belonging to his art,
His algorism stones- all laid apart
On shelves that ranged beside his lone bed's head;
His press was covered with a cloth of red.
And over all there lay a psaltery
Whereon he made an evening's melody,
Playing so sweetly that the chamber rang;
And Angelus ad virginem he sang;
And after that he warbled the King's Note:
Often in good voice was his merry throat.
And thus this gentle clerk his leisure spends
Supported by some income and his friends.
This carpenter had lately wed a wife
Whom lie loved better than he loved his life;
And she was come to eighteen years of age.
Jealous he was and held her close in cage.

For she was wild and young, and he was old,

And deemed himself as like to be cuckold.

He knew not Cato, for his lore was rude:

That vulgar man should wed similitude.

A man should wed according to estate,

For youth and age are often in debate.

But now, since he had fallen in the snare,

He must endure, like other folk, his care.

Fair was this youthful wife, and therewithal

As weasel's was her body slim and small.

A girdle wore she, barred and striped, of silk.

An apron, too, as white as morning milk

About her loins, and full of many a gore;

White was her smock, embroidered all before

And even behind, her collar round about,

Of coal-black silk, on both sides, in and out;

The strings of the white cap upon her head

Were, like her collar, black silk worked with thread,

Her fillet was of wide silk worn full high:

And certainly she had a lickerish eye.

She'd thinned out carefully her eyebrows two,

And they were arched and black as any sloe.

She was a far more pleasant thing to see

Than is the newly budded young pear-tree;

And softer than the wool is on a wether.

Down from her girdle hung a purse of leather,

Tasselled with silk, with latten beading sown.

In all this world, searching it up and down,

So gay a little doll, I well believe,

Or such a wench, there's no man can conceive.

Far brighter was the brilliance of her hue

Than in the Tower the gold coins minted new.

And songs came shrilling from her pretty head

As from a swallow's sitting on a shed.

Therewith she'd dance too, and could play and sham

Like any kid or calf about its dam.

Her mouth was sweet as bragget or as mead

Or hoard of apples laid in hay or weed.

Skittish she was as is a pretty colt,

Tall as a staff and straight as cross-bow bolt.

A brooch she wore upon her collar low,

As broad as boss of buckler did it show;

Her shoes laced up to where a girl's legs thicken.

She was a primrose, and a tender chicken

For any lord to lay upon his bed,

Or yet for any good yeoman to wed.

Now, sir, and then, sir, go befell the case,

That on a day this clever Nicholas

Fell in with this young wife to toy and play,

The while her husband was down Osney way,

Clerks being as crafty as the best of us;
And unperceived he caught her by the puss,
Saying: "Indeed, unless I have my will,
For secret love of you, sweetheart, I'll spill."
And held her hard about the hips, and how!
And said: "O darling, love me, love me now,
Or I shall die, and pray you God may save!"
And she leaped as a colt does in the trave,
And with her head she twisted fast away,
And said: "I will not kiss you, by my fay!
Why, let go," cried she, "let go, Nicholas!
Or I will call for help and cry 'alas!'
Do take your hands away, for courtesy!"
This Nicholas for mercy then did cry,
And spoke so well, importuned her so fast
That she her love did grant him at the last,
And swore her oath, by Saint Thomas of Kent,
That she would be at his command, content,
As soon as opportunity she could spy.
"My husband is so full of jealousy,
Unless you will await me secretly,
I know I'm just as good as dead," said she.
"You must keep all quite hidden in this case."
"Nay, thereof worry not," said Nicholas,
"A clerk has lazily employed his while

If he cannot a carpenter beguile."

And thus they were agreed, and then they swore

To wait a while, as I have said before.

When Nicholas had done thus every whit

And patted her about the loins a bit,

He kissed her sweetly, took his psaltery,

And played it fast and made a melody.

Then fell it thus, that to the parish kirk,

The Lord Christ Jesus' own works for to work,

This good wife went, upon a holy day;

Her forehead shone as bright as does the May,

So well she'd washed it when she left off work.

Now there was of that church a parish clerk

Whose name was (as folk called him) Absalom.

Curled was his hair, shining like gold, and from

His head spread fanwise in a thick bright mop;

'Twas parted straight and even on the top;

His cheek was red, his eyes grey as a goose;

With Saint Paul's windows cut upon his shoes,

He stood in red hose fitting famously.

And he was clothed full well and properly

All in a coat of blue, in which were let

Holes for the lacings, which were fairly set.

And over all he wore a fine surplice

As white as ever hawthorn spray, and nice.

A merry lad he was, so God me save,
And well could he let blood, cut hair, and shave,
And draw a deed or quitclaim, as might chance.
In twenty manners could he trip and dance,
After the school that reigned in Oxford, though,
And with his two legs swinging to and fro;
And he could play upon a violin;
Thereto he sang in treble voice and thin;
And as well could he play on his guitar.
In all the town no inn was, and no bar,
That he'd not visited to make good cheer,
Especially were lively barmaids there.
But, truth to tell, he was a bit squeamish
Of farting and of language haughtyish.
This Absalom, who was so light and gay,
Went with a censer on the holy day,
Censing the wives like an enthusiast;
And on them many a loving look he cast,
Especially on this carpenter's goodwife.
To look at her he thought a merry life,
She was so pretty, sweet, and lickerous.
I dare well say, if she had been a mouse
And he a cat, he would have mauled her some.
This parish clerk, this lively Absalom
Had in his heart, now, such a love-longing

That from no wife took he an offering;

For courtesy, he said, he would take none.

The moon, when it was night, full brightly shone,

And his guitar did Absalom then take,

For in love-watching he'd intent to wake.

And forth he went, jolly and amorous,

Until he came unto the carpenter's house

A little after cocks began to crow;

And took his stand beneath a shot-window

That was let into the good wood-wright's wall.

He sang then, in his pleasant voice and small,

"Oh now, dear lady, if your will it be,

I pray that you will have some ruth on me,"

The words in harmony with his string-plucking.

This carpenter awoke and heard him sing,

And called unto his wife and said, in sum:

"What, Alison! Do you hear Absalom,

Who plays and sings beneath our bedroom wall?"

And she said to her husband, therewithal:

"Yes, God knows, John, I bear it, truth to tell."

So this went on; what is there better than well?

From day to day this pretty Absalom

So wooed her he was woebegone therefrom.

He lay awake all night and all the day;

He combed his spreading hair and dressed him gay;

SIMON VAN BOOY

By go-betweens and agents, too, wooed he,

And swore her loyal page he'd ever be.

He sang as tremulously as nightingale;

He sent her sweetened wine and well-spiced ale

And waffles piping hot out of the fire,

And, she being town-bred, mead for her desire.

For some are won by means of money spent,

And some by tricks, and some by long descent.

Once, to display his versatility,

He acted Herod on a scaffold high.

But what availed it him in any case?

She was enamoured so of Nicholas

That Absalom might go and blow his horn;

He got naught for his labour but her scorn.

And thus she made of Absalom her ape,

And all his earnestness she made a jape.

For truth is in this proverb, and no lie,

Men say well thus: It's always he that's nigh

That makes the absent lover seem a sloth.

For now, though Absalom be wildly wroth,

Because he is so far out of her sight,

This handy Nicholas stands in his light.

Now bear you well, you clever Nicholas!

For Absalom may wail and sing "Alas!"

And so it chanced that on a Saturday

This carpenter departed to Osney;
And clever Nicholas and Alison
Were well agreed to this effect: anon
This Nicholas should put in play a wile
The simple, jealous husband to beguile;
And if it chanced the game should go a-right,
She was to sleep within his arms all night,
For this was his desire, and hers also.
Presently then, and without more ado,
This Nicholas, no longer did he tarry,
But softly to his chamber did he carry
Both food and drink to last at least a day,
Saying that to her husband she should say-
If he should come to ask for Nicholas-
Why, she should say she knew not where he was,
For all day she'd not seen him, far or nigh;
She thought he must have got some malady,
Because in vain her maid would knock and call;
He'd answer not, whatever might befall.
And so it was that all that Saturday
This Nicholas quietly in chamber lay,
And ate and slept, or did what pleased him best,
Till Sunday when the sun had gone to rest.
This simple man with wonder heard the tale,
And marvelled what their Nicholas might ail,

SIMON VAN BOOY

And said: "I am afraid, by Saint Thomas,

That everything's not well with Nicholas.

God send he be not dead so suddenly!

This world is most unstable, certainly;

I saw, today, the corpse being borne to kirk

Of one who, but last Monday, was at work.

"Go up," said he unto his boy anon,

"Call at his door, or knock there with a stone,

Learn how it is and boldly come tell me."

The servant went up, then, right sturdily,

And at the chamber door, the while he stood,

He cried and knocked as any madman would-

"What! How! What do you, Master Nicholay?

How can you sleep through all the livelong day?"

But all for naught, he never heard a word;

A hole he found, low down upon a board,

Through which the house cat had been wont to creep;

And to that hole he stooped, and through did peep,

And finally he ranged him in his sight.

This Nicholas sat gaping there, upright,

As if he'd looked too long at the new moon.

Downstairs he went and told his master soon

In what array he'd found this self-same man.

This carpenter to cross himself began,

And said: "Now help us, holy Frideswide!

Little a man can know what shall betide.

This man is fallen, with his astromy,

Into some madness or some agony;

I always feared that somehow this would be!

Men should not meddle in God's privity.

Aye, blessed always be the ignorant man,

Whose creed is, all he ever has to scan!

So fared another clerk with astromy;

He walked into the meadows for to pry

Into the stars, to learn what should befall,

Until into a clay-pit he did fall;

He saw not that. But yet, by Saint Thomas,

I'm sorry for this clever Nicholas.

He shall be scolded for his studying,

If not too late, by Jesus, Heaven's King!

"Get me a staff, that I may pry before,

The while you, Robin, heave against the door.

We'll take him from this studying, I guess."

And on the chamber door, then, he did press.

His servant was a stout lad, if a dunce,

And by the hasp he heaved it up at once;

Upon the floor that portal fell anon.

This Nicholas sat there as still as stone,

Gazing, with gaping mouth, straight up in air.

This carpenter thought he was in despair,

SIMON VAN BOOY

And took him by the shoulders, mightily,

And shook him hard, and cried out, vehemently:

"What! Nicholay! Why how now! Come, look down!

Awake, and think on Jesus' death and crown!

I cross you from all elves and magic wights!"

And then the night-spell said he out, by rights,

At the four corners of the house about,

And at the threshold of the door, without:-

"O Jesus Christ and good Saint Benedict,

Protect this house from all that may afflict,

For the night hag the white Paternoster!-

Where hast thou gone, Saint Peter's sister?"

And at the last this clever Nicholas

Began to sigh full sore, and said: "Alas!

Shall all the world be lost so soon again?"

This carpenter replied: "What say you, then?

What! Think on God, as we do, men that swink."

This Nicholas replied: "Go fetch me drink;

And afterward I'll tell you privately

A certain thing concerning you and me;

I'll tell it to no other man or men."

This carpenter went down and came again,

And brought of potent ale a brimming quart;

And when each one of them had drunk his part,

Nicholas shut the door fast, and with that

He drew a seat and near the carpenter sat.

He said: "Now, John, my good host, lief and dear,

You must upon your true faith swear, right here,

That to no man will you this word betray;

For it is Christ's own word that I will say,

And if you tell a man, you're ruined quite;

This punishment shall come to you, of right,

That if you're traitor you'll go mad- and should!"

"Nay, Christ forbid it, for His holy blood!"

Said then this simple man: "I am no blab,

Nor, though I say it, am I fond of gab.

Say what you will, I never will it tell

To child or wife, by Him that harried Hell!"

"Now, John," said Nicholas, "I will not lie;

But I've found out, from my astrology,

As I have looked upon the moon so bright,

That now, come Monday next, at nine of night,

Shall fall a rain so wildly mad as would

Have been, by half, greater than Noah's flood.

This world," he said, "in less time than an hour,

Shall all be drowned, so terrible is this shower;

Thus shall all mankind drown and lose all life."

This carpenter replied: "Alas, my wife!

And shall she drown? Alas, my Alison!"

For grief of this he almost fell. Anon

He said: "Is there no remedy in this case?"

"Why yes, good luck," said clever Nicholas,

"If you will work by counsel of the wise;

You must not act on what your wits advise.

For so says Solomon, and it's all true,

'Work by advice and thou shalt never rue.'

And if you'll act as counselled and not fail,

I undertake, without a mast or sail,

To save us all, aye you and her and me.

Haven't you heard of, Noah, how saved was he,

Because Our Lord had warned him how to keep

Out of the flood that covered earth so deep?"

"Yes," said this carpenter, "long years ago."

"Have you not heard," asked Nicholas, "also

The sorrows of Noah and his fellowship

In getting his wife to go aboard the ship?

He would have rather, I dare undertake,

At that time, and for all the weather black,

That she had one ship for herself alone.

Therefore, do you know what would best be done?

This thing needs haste, and of a hasty thing

Men must not preach nor do long tarrying.

"Presently go, and fetch here to this inn

A kneading-tub, or brewing vat, and win

One each for us, but see that they are large,

Wherein we may swim out as in a barge,

And have therein sufficient food and drink

For one day only; that's enough, I think.

The water will dry up and flow away

About the prime of the succeeding day.

But Robin must not know of this, your knave,

And even Jill, your maid, I may not save;

Ask me not why, for though you do ask me,

I will not tell you of God's privity.

Suffice you, then, unless your wits are mad,

To have as great a grace as Noah had.

Your wife I shall not lose, there is no doubt,

Go, now, your way, and speedily about,

But when you have, for you and her and me,

Procured these kneading-tubs, or beer-vats, three,

Then you shall hang them near the roof-tree high,

That no man our purveyance may espy.

And when you thus have done, as I have said,

And have put in our drink and meat and bread,

Also an axe to cut the ropes in two

When the flood comes, that we may float and go,

And cut a hole, high up, upon the gable,

Upon the garden side, over the stable,

That we may freely pass forth on our way

When the great rain and flood are gone that day-

SIMON VAN BOOY

Then shall you float as merrily, I'll stake,

As does the white duck after the white drake.

Then I will call, 'Ho, Alison! Ho, John!

Be cheery, for the flood will pass anon.'

And you will say, 'Hail. Master Nicholay!

Good morrow, I see you well, for it is day!'

And then shall we be barons all our life

Of all the world, like Noah and his wife.

"But of one thing I warn you now, outright.

Be well advised, that on that very night

When we have reached our ships and got aboard,

Not one of us must speak or whisper word,

Nor call, nor cry, but sit in silent prayer;

For this is God's own bidding, hence- don't dare!

"Your wife and you must hang apart, that in

The night shall come no chance for you to sin

Either in looking or in carnal deed.

These orders I have told you, go, God speed!

Tomorrow night, when all men are asleep,

Into our kneading-tubs will we three creep

And sit there, still, awaiting God's high grace.

Go, now, your way, I have no longer space

Of time to make a longer sermoning.

Men say thus: 'Send the wise and say no thing.'

You are so wise it needs not that I teach;

Go, save our lives, and that I do beseech."

This silly carpenter went on his way.

Often he cried "Alas!" and "Welaway!"

And to his wife he told all, privately;

But she was better taught thereof than he

How all this rigmarole was to apply.

Nevertheless she acted as she'd die,

And said: "Alas! Go on your way anon,

help us escape, or we are lost, each one;

I am your true and lawfully wedded wife;

Go, my dear spouse, and help to save our life."

Lo, what a great thing is affection found!

Men die of imagination, I'll be bound,

So deep an imprint may the spirit take.

This hapless carpenter began to quake;

He thought now, verily, that he could see

Old Noah's flood come wallowing like the sea

To drown his Alison, his honey dear.

He wept, he wailed, he made but sorry cheer,

He sighed and made full many a sob and sough.

He went and got himself a kneading-trough

And, after that, two tubs he somewhere found

And to his dwelling privately sent round,

And hung them near the roof, all secretly.

With his own hand, then, made he ladders three,

To climb up by the rungs thereof, it seems,

And reach the tubs left hanging to the beams;

And those he victualled, tubs and kneading-trough,

With bread and cheese and good jugged ale, enough

To satisfy the needs of one full day.

But ere he'd put all this in such array,

He sent his servants, boy and maid, right down

Upon some errand into London town.

And on the Monday, when it came on night,

He shut his door, without a candle-light,

And ordered everything as it should be.

And shortly after up they climbed, all three;

They sat while one might plow a furlong-way.

"Now, by Our Father, hush!" said Nicholay,

And "Hush!" said John, and "Hush!" said Alison.

This carpenter, his loud devotions done,

Sat silent, saying mentally a prayer,

And waiting for the rain, to hear it there.

The deathlike sleep of utter weariness

Fell on this wood-wright even. (as I guess)

About the curfew time, or little more;

For travail of his spirit he groaned sore,

And soon he snored, for badly his head lay.

Down by the ladder crept this Nicholay,

And Alison, right softly down she sped.

Without more words they went and got in bed

Even where the carpenter was wont to lie.

There was the revel and the melody!

And thus lie Alison and Nicholas,

In joy that goes by many an alias,

Until the bells for lauds began to ring

And friars to the chancel went to sing.

This parish clerk, this amorous Absalom,

Whom love has made so woebegone and dumb,

Upon the Monday was down Osney way,

With company, to find some sport and play;

And there he chanced to ask a cloisterer,

Privately, after John the carpenter.

This monk drew him apart, out of the kirk,

And said: "I have not seen him here at work.

Since Saturday; I think well that he went

For timber, that the abbot has him sent;

For he is wont for timber thus to go,

Remaining at the grange a day or so;

Or else he's surely at his house today;

But which it is I cannot truly say."

This Absalom right happy was and light,

And thought: "Now is the time to wake all night;

For certainly I saw him not stirring

About his door since day began to spring.

SIMON VAN BOOY

So may I thrive, as I shall, at cock's crow,
Knock cautiously upon that window low
Which is so placed upon his bedroom wall.
To Alison then will I tell of all
My love-longing, and thus I shall not miss
That at the least I'll have her lips to kiss.
Some sort of comfort shall I have, I say,
My mouth's been itching all this livelong day;
That is a sign of kissing at the least.
All night I dreamed, too, I was at a feast.
Therefore I'll go and sleep two hours away
And all this night then will I wake and play."
And so when time of first cock-crow was come,
Up rose this merry lover, Absalom,
And dressed him gay and all at point-device,
But first he chewed some licorice and spice
So he'd smell sweet, ere he had combed his hair.
Under his tongue some bits of true-love rare,
For thereby thought he to be more gracious.
He went, then, to the carpenter's dark house.
And silent stood beneath the shot-window;
Unto his breast it reached, it was so low;
And he coughed softly, in a low half tone:
"What do you, honeycomb, sweet Alison?
My cinnamon, my fair bird, my sweetie,

Awake, O darling mine, and speak to me!

It's little thought you give me and my woe,

Who for your love do sweat where'er I go.

Yet it's no wonder that I faint and sweat;

I long as does the lamb for mother's teat.

Truly, sweetheart, I have such love-longing

That like a turtle-dove's my true yearning;

And I can eat no more than can a maid."

"Go from the window, Jack-a-napes," she said,

"For, s'help me God, it is not 'come kiss me.'

I love another, or to blame I'd be,

Better than you, by Jesus, Absalom!

Go on your way, or I'll stone you therefrom,

And let me sleep, the fiends take you away!"

"Alas," quoth Absalom, "and welaway!

That true love ever was so ill beset!

But kiss me, since you'll do no more, my pet,

For Jesus' love and for the love of me."

"And will you go, then, on your way?" asked she,

"Yes truly, darling," said this Absalom.

"Then make you ready," said she, "and I'll come!"

And unto Nicholas said she, low and still:

"Be silent now, and you shall laugh your fill."

This Absalom plumped down upon his knees,

And said: "I am a lord in all degrees;

For after this there may be better still

Darling, my sweetest bird, I wait your will."

The window she unbarred, and that in haste.

"Have done," said she, "come on, and do it fast,

Before we're seen by any neighbour's eye."

This Absalom did wipe his mouth all dry;

Dark was the night as pitch, aye dark as coal,

And through the window she put out her hole.

And Absalom no better felt nor worse,

But with his mouth he kissed her naked arse

Right greedily, before he knew of this.

Aback he leapt- it seemed somehow amiss,

For well he knew a woman has no beard;

He'd felt a thing all rough and longish haired,

And said, "Oh fie, alas! What did I do?"

"Teehee!" she laughed, and clapped the window to;

And Absalom went forth a sorry pace.

"A beard! A beard!" cried clever Nicholas,

"Now by God's corpus, this goes fair and well!"

This hapless Absalom, he heard that yell,

And on his lip, for anger, he did bite;

And to himself he said, "I will requite!"

Who vigorously rubbed and scrubbed his lips

With dust, with sand, with straw, with cloth, with chips,

But Absalom, and often cried "Alas!

My soul I give now unto Sathanas,

For rather far than own this town," said he,

"For this despite, it's well revenged I'd be.

Alas," said he, "from her I never blenched!"

His hot love was grown cold, aye and all quenched;

For, from the moment that he'd kissed her arse,

For paramours he didn't care a curse,

For he was healed of all his malady;

Indeed all paramours he did defy,

And wept as does a child that has been beat.

With silent step he went across the street

Unto a smith whom men called Dan Jarvis,

Who in his smithy forged plow parts, that is

He sharpened shares and coulters busily.

This Absalom he knocked all easily,

And said: "Unbar here, Jarvis, for I come."

"What! Who are you?"

"It's I, it's Absalom."

"What! Absalom! For Jesus Christ's sweet tree,

Why are you up so early? Ben'cite!

What ails you now, man? Some gay girl, God knows,

Has brought you on the jump to my bellows;

By Saint Neot, you know well what I mean."

This Absalom cared not a single bean

For all this play, nor one word back he gave;

He'd more tow on his distaff, had this knave,

Than Jarvis knew, and said he: "Friend so dear,

This red-hot coulter in the fireplace here,

Lend it to me, I have a need for it,

And I'll return it after just a bit."

Jarvis replied: "Certainly, were it gold

Or a purse filled with yellow coins untold,

Yet should you have it, as I am true smith;

But eh, Christ's foe! What will you do therewith?"

"Let that," said Absalom, "be as it may;

I'll tell you all tomorrow, when it's day"—

And caught the coulter then by the cold steel

And softly from the smithy door did steal

And went again up to the wood-wright's wall.

He coughed at first, and then he knocked withal

Upon the window, as before, with care.

This Alison replied: "Now who is there?

And who knocks so? I'll warrant it's a thief."

"Why no," quoth he, "God knows, my sweet roseleaf,

I am your Absalom, my own darling!

Of gold," quoth he, "I have brought you a ring;

My mother gave it me, as I'll be saved;

Fine gold it is, and it is well engraved;

This will I give you for another kiss."

This Nicholas had risen for a piss,

And thought that it would carry on the jape
To have his arse kissed by this jack-a-nape.
And so he opened window hastily,
And put his arse out thereat, quietly,
Over the buttocks, showing the whole bum;
And thereto said this clerk, this Absalom,
"O speak, sweet bird, I know not where thou art."
This Nicholas just then let fly a fart
As loud as it had been a thunder-clap,
And well-nigh blinded Absalom, poor chap;
But he was ready with his iron hot
And Nicholas right in the arse he got.
Off went the skin a hand's-breadth broad, about,
The coulter burned his bottom so, throughout,
That for the pain he thought that he should die.
And like one mad he started in to cry,
"help! Water! Water! For God's dear heart!"
This carpenter out of his sleep did start,
Hearing that "Water!" cried as madman would,
And thought, "Alas, now comes down Noel's flood!"
He struggled up without another word
And with his axe he cut in two the cord,
And down went all; he did not stop to trade
In bread or ale till he'd the journey made,
And there upon the floor he swooning lay.

Up started Alison and Nicholay
And shouted "help!" and "Hello!" down the street.
The neighbours, great and small, with hastening feet
Swarmed in the house to stare upon this man,
Who lay yet swooming, and all pale and wan;
For in the falling he had smashed his arm.
He had to suffer, too, another harm,
For when he spoke he was at once borne down
By clever Nicholas and Alison.
For they told everyone that he was odd;
He was so much afraid of "Noel's" flood,
Through fantasy, that out of vanity
He'd gone and bought these kneading-tubs, all three,
And that he'd hung them near the roof above;
And that he had prayed them, for God's dear love,
To sit with him and bear him company.
The people laughed at all this fantasy;
Up to the roof they looked, and there did gape,
And so turned all his injury to a jape.
For when this carpenter got in a word,
'Twas all in vain, no man his reasons heard;
With oaths imprenive he was so sworn down,
That he was held for mad by all the town;
For every clerk did side with every other.
They said: "The man is crazy, my dear brother."

And everyone did laugh at all this strife.

Thus futtered was the carpenter's goodwife,

For all his watching and his jealousy;

And Absalom has kissed her nether eye;

And Nicholas is branded on the butt.

This tale is done, and God save all the rout!

Jean-Baptiste Greuze, *Broken Eggs*, 1756

Emily Dickinson was born in 1830 to a prosperous family in Amherst, Massachusetts. The Dickinson house was alight with ambition, both legal and political; however, the world of her father was not one Dickinson took much interest in. She preferred gardening, baking, reading, playing the piano, and taking walks. Despite a single year at a female seminary and the occasional trip to Boston to see an optician, she barely left the house.

When she died in her mid-fifties, she left behind almost two thousand poems, only a few of which were published during her lifetime.

Emily Dickinson

"Wild nights—Wild nights!"

Wild nights—Wild nights!
Were I with thee
Wild nights should be
Our luxury!

Futile—the winds—
To a Heart in port—
Done with the Compass—
Done with the Chart!

Rowing in Eden—
Ah—the Sea!
Might I but moor—tonight—
In thee!

Katsushika Hokusai, *Ejiri in Suruga Province,* 1830–33

Desmond Morris was born in England in 1928 and is a popular British zoologist. Prior to the wide success of his book *The Naked Ape*, published in 1967, Morris worked as a television presenter for *The World of Animals*, *Zoo Time*, and *The Animal Story*. His later works, which include a sequel to The Naked Ape, continued to explore human behavior from a zoological perspective.

When *The Naked Ape* was published nearly fifty years ago, it caused an enormous amount of controversy, as it described human beings in the same way as a zoologist portrays animals.

Desmond Morris

from the chapter "Sex" from *The Naked Ape*

Sexual behaviour in our species goes through three charac-
teristic phases: pair-formation, pre-copulatory activity, and
copulation, usually but not always in that order. The pair-
formation stage, usually referred to as courtship, is remark-
ably prolonged by animal standards, frequently lasting for
weeks or even months. As with many other species it is char-
acterized by tentative, ambivalent behaviour involving con-
flicts between fear, aggression and sexual attraction. The
nervousness and hesitancy is slowly reduced if the mutual
sexual signals are strong enough. These involve complex facial
expressions, body postures and vocalizations. The latter in-
volve the highly specialized and symbolized sound signals of
speech, but equally importantly they present to the member
of the opposite sex a distinctive vocalization tone. A court-
ing couple is often referred to as "murmuring sweet nothings"
and this phrase sums up clearly the significance of the tone of
voice as opposed to what is being spoken.

After the initial stages of visual and vocal display, simple
body contacts are made. These usually accompany locomo-
tion, which is now considerably increased when the pair are
together. Hand-to-hand and arm-to-arm contacts are fol-
lowed by mouth-to-face and mouth-to-mouth ones. Mutual

embracing occurs, both statically and during locomotion. Sudden spontaneous outbursts of running, chasing, jumping and dancing are commonly seen and juvenile play patterns may reappear.

Much of this pair-formation phase may take place in public, but when it passes over into the pre-copulatory phase, privacy is sought and the subsequent patterns of behaviour are performed in isolation from other members of the species as far as is possible. With the pre-copulatory stage there is a striking increase in the adoption of a horizontal posture. Body-to-body contacts are increased in both force and duration. Low-intensity side-by-side postures repeatedly give way to high-intensity face-to-face contacts. These positions may be maintained for many minutes and even for several hours, during which vocal and visual signals become gradually less important and tactile signals increasingly frequent. These involve small movements and varying pressures from all parts of the body, but in particular from the fingers, hands, lips and tongue. Clothing is partially or totally removed and skin-to-skin tactile stimulation is increased over as wide an area as possible.

Now that we have all these facts before us we can start to ask questions. How does the way we behave sexually help us to survive? Why do we behave in the way we do, rather than in some other way? We may be helped in these questions if we ask another one: How does our sexual behaviour compare with that of other living primates?

Straight away we can see that there is much more intense sexual activity in our own species than in any other primates, including our closest relations. For them, the lengthy courtship phase is missing.

Hardly any of the monkeys and apes develop a prolonged pair-bond relationship. The pre-copulatory patterns are brief and usually consist of no more than a few facial expressions and simple vocalizations. Copulation itself is also very brief. (In baboons, for instance, the time taken from mounting to ejaculation is no more than seven to eight seconds, with a total of no more than fifteen pelvic thrusts, often fewer.) The female does not appear to experience any kind of climax. If there is anything that could be called an orgasm it is a trivial response when compared with that of the female of our own species.

The period of sexual receptivity of the female monkey or ape is more restricted. It usually only lasts for about a week, or a little more, of their monthly cycle. Even this is an advance on the lower mammals, where it is limited more severely to the actual time of ovulation, but in our own species the primate trend towards longer receptivity has been pushed to the very limit, so that the female is receptive at virtually all times.

Once a female monkey or ape becomes pregnant, or is nursing a baby, she ceases to be sexually active. Again, our species has spread its sexual activities into these periods, so that there is only a brief time just before and just after parturition when mating is seriously limited.

Clearly, the naked ape is the sexiest primate alive. To find the reason for this we have to look back again at his origins. What happened? First, he had to hunt if he was to survive. Second, he had to have a better brain to make up for his poor hunting body. Third, he had to have a longer childhood to grow the bigger brain and to educate it. Fourth, the females had to stay put and mind the babies while the males went hunting. Fifth, the males had to co-operate with one another on the hunt. Sixth, they had to stand up straight and use weapons for the hunt to succeed. I am not implying that these changes happened in that order; on the contrary they undoubtedly all developed gradually at the same time, each modification helping the others along. I am simply enumerating the six basic, major changes that took place as the hunting ape evolved. Inherent in these changes there are, I believe, all the ingredients necessary to make up our present sexual complexity.

To begin with, the males had to be sure that their females were going to be faithful to them when they left them alone to go hunting. So the females had to develop a pairing tendency. Also, if the weaker males were going to be expected to co-operate on the hunt, they had to be given more sexual rights. The females would have to be more shared out, the sexual organization more democratic, less tyrannical. Each male, too, would need a strong pairing tendency. Furthermore, the males were now armed with deadly weapons and sexual rivalries would be much more dangerous: again, a good reason for each male being satisfied with one female. On top of that there were the much heavier parental demands being made by the slow-growing infants. Paternal behaviour would have to be developed and the parental duties shared between the mother and the father: another good reason for a strong pair-bond.

Given this situation as a starting point we can now see how other things grew from it. The naked ape had to develop the capacity for falling in love, for becoming sexually imprinted on a single partner, for evolving a pair-bond. Whichever way you put it, it comes to the same thing. How did he manage to do this? What were the factors that helped him undo this trend? As a primate, he will already have had a tendency to form brief mateships lasting a few hours, or perhaps even a few days, but these now had to be intensified and extended. One thing that will have come to his aid is his own prolonged childhood. During the long, growing years he will have had the chance to develop a deep personal relationship with his parents, a relationship much more powerful and lasting than anything a young monkey could experience. The loss of this parental bond with maturation and independence would create a "relationship void"—a gap that had to be filled. He would therefore already be primed for the development of a new, equally powerful bond to replace it.

Even if this was enough to intensify his need for forming a new pair-bond, there would still have to be additional assistance to maintain it. It would have to last long enough for the lengthy process of rearing a family. Having fallen in love, he would have to stay in love. By developing a prolonged and exciting courtship phase he could ensure the former, but something more would be needed after that. The simplest and most direct method of doing this was to make the shared activities of the pair more complicated and more rewarding. In other words, to make sex sexier.

How was this done? In every possible way, seems to be the answer. If we look back now at the behaviour of the present-day naked ape we can see the pattern taking shape. The increased receptivity of the female cannot be explained only in terms of increasing the birth-rate. It is true that by being prepared to copulate while still at the maternal phase of rearing a baby, the female does increase the birth-rate. With the very long dependency period, it would be a disaster if she did not. But this cannot explain why she is ready to receive the male and become sexually aroused throughout each of her monthly cycles. She only ovulates at one point during the cycle, so that mating at all other times can have no procreative function. The vast bulk of copulation in our species is obviously concerned, not with producing offspring, but with cementing the pair-bond by providing mutual rewards for the sexual partners. The repeated attainment of sexual consummation for a mated pair is clearly, then, not some kind of sophisticated, decadent outgrowth of modern civilization, but a deep-rooted, biologically based, and evolutionarily sound tendency of our species.

Even when she has stopped going through her monthly cycles—in other words, when she is pregnant—the female remains responsive to the male. This, too, is particularly important because, with a one-male-one-female system, it would be dangerous to frustrate the male for too long a period. It might endanger the pair-bond.

In addition to increasing the amount of time when sexual activities can take place, the activities themselves have been elaborated. The hunting life that gave us naked skins and more sensitive hands has given us much greater scope for sexually stimulating body-to-body contacts. During pre-copulatory behaviour these play a major role. Stroking, rubbing, pressing and caressing occur in abundance and far exceed anything found in other primate species.

Also, specialized organs such as the lips, ear-lobes, nipples, breasts and genitals are richly endowed with nerve-endings and have become highly sensitized to erotic tactile stimulation. The ear-lobes, indeed, appear to have been exclusively evolved to this end. Anatomists have often referred to them as meaningless appendages, or "useless, fatty excrescences." In general parlance they are explained away as "remnants" of the time when we had big ears. But if we look at other primate species, we find that they do not possess fleshy ear-lobes. It seems that, far from being a remnant, they are something new, and when we discover that, under the influence of sexual arousal, they become engorged with blood, swollen and hypersensitive, there can be little doubt that their evolution has been exclusively concerned with the production of yet another erogenous zone.

This, then, is the naked ape in all its erotic complexity: a highly sexed, pair-forming species with many unique features; a complicated blend of primate ancestry with extensive carnivore modifications. Now, to this we must add the third and final ingredient: modern civilization. The enlarged brain that accompanied the transformation of the simple forest-dweller into a co-operative hunter began to busy itself with technological improvements. The simple tribal dwelling places became great towns and cities. The axe age blossomed into the space age. But what effect did the acquisition of all this

SIMON VAN BOOY

gloss and glitter have on the sexual system of the species? Very little, seems to be the answer. It has all been too quick, too sudden, for any fundamental biological advances to occur. Superficially they *seem* to have occurred, it is true, but this is largely make-believe. Behind the façade of modern city life there is the same old naked ape. Only the names have been changed: for "hunting" read "working," for "hunting grounds" read "place of business," for "home base" read "house," for "pair-bond" read "marriage," for "mate" read "wife," and so on.

Sensuality often makes love grow too quickly, so that the root remains weak and is easy to pull out.

—*Friedrich Nietzsche*

Dr. Theodor Reik was born in 1888 in Vienna, but became an American citizen in 1944 after fleeing the Nazis. Reik studied with Freud for several years and authored many books on diverse subjects relating to psychoanalysis, including *The Unknown Murderer*, *Pagan Rites in Judaism*, and *The Compulsion to Confess*. Freud knew Reik as a brilliant student and helped him as a young man overcome the crippling neuroses caused by his father's death when Reik was only eighteen years old. Reik died in 1969.

Theodor Reik

from *The Need to Be Loved*

The girl who daydreamed (as a child) that Prince Charming would come on his white steed to marry her is perhaps ecstatically happy when that flatfooted salesman arrives on the train from Chicago and proposes to her. He is Prince Charming for her, and no one derives greater happiness than this girl when she can show off her engagement ring to her friends. She and her salesman fiancé, exuberant with joy about his achievement, have experienced the fulfillment of their childhood wishes, however modified and qualified. They still live in the world of fairy tales.

How little is needed to make people happy! We think of that minimum of satisfaction of the need to be loved and it makes us wonder. It sounds like the refrain of a song.

Happiness is restricted to hours, if not to minutes, and can be sometimes easily achieved; but to achieve enduring contentment is quite another matter.

Vincent Van Gogh was a Dutch painter born in 1853. He had an older brother, also called Vincent Van Gogh, who died at birth. Largely self-taught as a painter, Van Gogh worked many odd jobs in his life, which provided some of the inspiration for his vibrant paintings, famous for their unique brushstroke and vivid colors. He suffered from a form of epilepsy, and his obsession with hard work and late nights undermined his fragile mental state. Throughout his life, Van Gogh kept a regular correspondence with his brother, Theo, and his feelings and struggles are chronicled in three published volumes totaling about eight hundred letters. He committed suicide in a wheat field in his late thirties, believing that his life as a painter had been a failure. Theo died a few months later. After the death of the Van Gogh brothers, Theo Van Gogh's wife devoted her life to getting her brother-in-law the attention she felt he deserved. In his lifetime, Vincent Van Gogh sold one painting.

In Van Gogh's *Siesta*, two people are doing nothing on a day of no particular significance. But when viewed within the context of love and companionship, it becomes a symbol of the profound sense of peace and joy that a happy union can bring about.

Vincent Van Gogh, *Siesta*, 1889–90

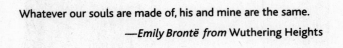

Whatever our souls are made of, his and mine are the same.

—*Emily Brontë from* Wuthering Heights

Pierre Paul Proudhon, *Innocence Preferring Love to Wealth,*
1804

True love is like ghosts, which everyone talks about and few have seen.

—*François de La Rochefoucauld*

Erich Fromm was born in Germany in 1900, and moved to the United States in 1934 where he lived for the next four decades. He was a psychoanalyst and a philosopher.

In his book *The Art of Loving*, Fromm examines the various kinds of love, and suggests ways people can overcome obstacles that may prevent them experiencing the full spectrum of love. In this extract, Fromm raises the question of whether love is something that just happens to us, or whether loving is actually an act of will.

Erich Fromm

"Erotic Love" from *The Art of Loving*

Brotherly love is love among equals; motherly love is love for the helpless. Different as they are from each other, they have in common that they are by their very nature not restricted to one person. If I love my brother, I love all my brothers; if I love my child, I love all my children; no, beyond that, I love all children, all that are in need of my help. In contrast to both types of love is *erotic love*; it is the craving for complete fusion, for union with one other person. It is by its very nature exclusive and not universal; it is also perhaps the most deceptive form of love there is.

First of all, it is often confused with the explosive experience of "falling" in love, the sudden collapse of the barriers which existed until that moment between two strangers. But, as was pointed out before, this experience of sudden intimacy is by its very nature short-lived. After the stranger has become an intimately known person there are no more barriers to be overcome, there is no more sudden closeness to be achieved. The "loved" person becomes as well known as oneself. Or, perhaps I should better say as little known. If there were more depth in the experience of the other person, if one could experience the infiniteness of his personality, the other person would never be so familiar—and the miracle of overcoming the barriers might occur every day anew. But for most people their own person, as well as others, is soon explored and soon exhausted. For them intimacy is established primarily through sexual contact. Since they experience the separateness of the other person primarily as physical separateness, physical union means overcoming separateness.

Beyond that, there are other factors which to many people denote the overcoming of separateness. To speak of one's own personal life, one's hopes and anxieties, to show oneself with one's childlike or childish aspects, to establish a common interest vis-à-vis the world—all this is taken as overcoming separateness. Even to show one's anger, one's hate, one's complete lack of inhibition is taken for intimacy, and this may explain the perverted attraction married couples often have for each other, who seem intimate only when they are in bed or when they give vent to their mutual hate and rage. But all these types of closeness tend to become reduced more and more as time goes on. The consequence is one seeks love with a new person, with a new stranger. Again the stranger is transformed into an "intimate" person, again the experience of falling in love is exhilarating and intense, and again it slowly becomes less and less intense, and ends in the wish for a new conquest, a new love—always with the illusion that the new love will be different from the earlier ones. These illusions are greatly helped by the deceptive character of sexual desire.

Sexual desire aims at fusion—and is by no means only a physical appetite, the relief of a painful tension. But sexual desire can be stimulated by the anxiety of aloneness, by the wish to conquer or be conquered, by vanity, by the wish to hurt and even to destroy, as much as it can be stimulated by love. It seems that sexual desire can easily blend with and be stimulated by any strong emotion, of which love is only one. Because sexual desire is in the minds of most people coupled with the idea of love, they are easily misled to conclude that they love each other when they want each other physically. Love can inspire the wish for sexual union; in this case the physical relationship is lacking in greediness, in a wish to conquer or to be conquered, but is blended with tenderness. If the desire for physical union is not stimulated by love, if erotic love is not also brotherly love, it never leads to union in more than an orgiastic, transitory sense. Sexual attraction creates, for the moment, the illusion of union, yet without love this "union" leaves strangers as far apart as they were before—sometimes it makes them ashamed of each other, or even makes them hate each other, because when the illusion has gone they feel their estrangement even more markedly than before. Tenderness is by no means, as Freud believed, a sublimation of the sexual instinct; it is the direct outcome of brotherly love, and exists in physical as well as in nonphysical forms of love.

In erotic love there is an exclusiveness which is lacking in brotherly love and motherly love. This exclusive character of erotic love warrants some further discussion. Frequently the exclusiveness of erotic love is misinterpreted as meaning possessive attachment. One can often find two people "in love" with each other who feel no love for anybody else. Their love is, in fact, an egotism *à deux*; they are two people who identify themselves with each other, and who solve the problem of separateness by enlarging the single individual into two. They have the experience of overcoming aloneness, yet, since they are separated from the rest of mankind, they remain separated from each other and alienated from themselves; their experience of union is an illusion.

Erotic love is exclusive, but it loves in the other person all of mankind, all that is alive. It is exclusive only in the sense that I can fuse myself fully and intensely with one person only. Erotic love excludes the love for others only in the sense of erotic fusion, full commitment in all aspects of life—but not in the sense of deep brotherly love.

Erotic love, if it is love, has one premise. That I love from the essence of my being—and experience the other person in the essence of his or her being. In essence, all human beings are identical. We are all part of One; we are One. This being so, it should not make any difference whom we love. Love should be essentially an act of will, of decision to commit my life completely to that of one other person. This is, indeed, the rationale behind the idea of the insolubility of marriage, as it is behind the many forms of traditional marriage in which the two partners never choose each other, but are chosen for each other—and yet are expected to love each other. In contemporary Western culture this idea appears altogether false. Love is supposed to be the outcome of a spontaneous, emotional reaction, of suddenly being gripped by an irresistible feeling. In this view, one sees only the peculiarities of the two individuals involved—and not the fact that all men are part of Adam, and all women part of Eve. One neglects to see an important factor in erotic love, that of *will*. To love somebody is not just a strong feeling—it is a decision, it is a judgment, it is a promise. If love were only a feeling, there would be no basis for the promise to love each other forever. A feeling comes and it may go. How can I judge that it will stay forever, when my act does not involve judgment and decision?

Taking these views into account one may arrive at the position that love is exclusively an act of will and commitment, and that therefore fundamentally it does not matter who the two persons are. Whether the marriage was arranged by others, or the result of individual choice, once the marriage is concluded, the act of will should guarantee the continuation of love. This view seems to neglect the paradoxical character of human nature and of erotic love. We are all One—yet every one of us is a unique, unduplicable entity. In our relationships to others the same paradox is repeated. Inasmuch as we are all one, we can love everybody in the same way in the sense of brotherly love. But inasmuch as we are all also different, erotic love requires certain specific, highly individual elements which exist between some people but not between all.

Both views then, that of erotic love as completely individual attraction, unique between two specific persons, as well as the other view that erotic love is nothing but an act of will, are true—or, as it may be put more aptly, the truth is neither this nor that. Hence the idea of a relationship which can be easily dissolved if one is not successful with it is as erroneous as the idea that under no circumstances must the relationship be dissolved.

In 1882 James Joyce was born in Ireland, "one of six-teen or seventeen children" according to his father (the eldest of ten in real life). He lived most of his life in self-imposed exile in Zurich and Paris—where he scraped a living together teaching English. Joyce also relied on the generosity of friends and patrons who believed in his work and supported him wholeheartedly.

In the summer of 1904, when Joyce was twenty-two, he met a girl named Nora Barnacle, a chambermaid at Finn's Hotel in Dublin. They had two children and were to remain together until Joyce's death in 1941.

Joyce's literary life was not easy, and his attempts to publish were often fraught with struggle and legal intervention. In 1922, five hundred copies of *Ulysses* were burned by the U.S. Department of the Post Office. Many scholars believe that the publication of Joyce's *Ulysses* changed the course of Western literature.

James Joyce

"A Painful Case" from *Dubliners*

Mr. James Duffy lived in Chapelizod because he wished to live as far as possible from the city of which he was a citizen and because he found all the other suburbs of Dublin mean, modern and pretentious. He lived in an old sombre house and from his windows he could look into the disused distillery or upwards along the shallow river on which Dublin is built. The lofty walls of his uncarpeted room were free from pictures. He had himself bought every article of furniture in the room: a black iron bedstead, an iron washstand, four cane chairs, a clothes-rack, a coalscuttle, a fender and irons and a square table on which lay a double desk. A bookcase had been made in an alcove by means of shelves of white wood. The bed was clothed with white bedclothes and a black and scarlet rug covered the foot. A little hand-mirror hung above the washstand and during the day a white-shaded lamp stood as the sole ornament of the mantelpiece. The books on the white wooden shelves were arranged from below upwards according to bulk. A complete Wordsworth stood at one end of the lowest shelf and a copy of the *Maynooth Catechism*, sewn into the cloth cover of a notebook, stood at one end of the top shelf. Writing materials were always on the desk. In the desk lay a manuscript translation of Hauptmann's

Michael Kramer, the stage directions of which were written in purple ink, and a little sheaf of papers held together by a brass pin. In these sheets a sentence was inscribed from time to time and, in an ironical moment, the headline of an advertisement for *Bile Beans* had been pasted on to the first sheet. On lifting the lid of the desk a faint fragrance escaped—the fragrance of new cedarwood pencils or of a bottle of gum or of an overripe apple which might have been left there and forgotten.

Mr. Duffy abhorred anything which betokened physical or mental disorder. A mediaeval doctor would have called him saturnine. His face, which carried the entire tale of his years, was of the brown tint of Dublin streets. On his long and rather large head grew dry black hair and a tawny moustache did not quite cover an unamiable mouth. His cheekbones also gave his face a harsh character; but there was no harshness in the eyes which, looking at the world from under their tawny eyebrows, gave the impression of a man ever alert to greet a redeeming instinct in others but often disappointed. He lived at a little distance from his body, regarding his own acts with doubtful side-glances. He had an odd autobiographical habit which led him to compose in his mind from time to time a short sentence about himself containing a subject in the third person and a predicate in the past tense. He never gave alms to beggars and walked firmly, carrying a stout hazel.

SIMON VAN BOOY

He had been for many years cashier of a private bank in Baggot Street. Every morning he came in from Chapelizod by tram. At midday he went to Dan Burke's and took his lunch—a bottle of lager beer and a small trayful of arrowroot biscuits. At four o'clock he was set free. He dined in an eating-house in George's Street where he felt himself safe from the society of Dublin's gilded youth and where there was a certain plain honesty in the bill of fare. His evenings were spent either before his landlady's piano or roaming about the outskirts of the city. His liking for Mozart's music brought him sometimes to an opera or a concert: these were the only dissipations of his life.

He had neither companions nor friends, church nor creed. He lived his spiritual life without any communion with others, visiting his relatives at Christmas and escorting them to the cemetery when they died. He performed these two social duties for old dignity's sake but conceded nothing further to the conventions which regulate the civic life. He allowed himself to think that in certain circumstances he would rob his bank but, as these circumstances never arose, his life rolled out evenly—an adventureless tale.

One evening he found himself sitting beside two ladies in the Rotunda. The house, thinly peopled and silent, gave distressing prophecy of failure. The lady who sat next to him looked round at the deserted house once or twice and then said:

"What a pity there is such a poor house tonight! It's so hard on people to have to sing to empty benches."

He took the remark as an invitation to talk. He was surprised that she seemed so little awkward. While they talked he tried to fix her permanently in his memory. When he learned that the young girl beside her was her daughter he judged her to be a year or so younger than himself. Her face, which must have been handsome, had remained intelligent. It was an oval face with strongly marked features. The eyes were very dark blue and steady. Their gaze began with a defiant note but was confused by what seemed a deliberate swoon of the pupil into the iris, revealing for an instant a temperament of great sensibility. The pupil reasserted itself quickly, this half-disclosed nature fell again under the reign of prudence, and her astrakhan jacket, moulding a bosom of a certain fulness, struck the note of defiance more definitely.

He met her again a few weeks afterwards at a concert in Earlsfort Terrace and seized the moments when her daughter's attention was diverted to become intimate. She alluded once or twice to her husband but her tone was not such as to make the allusion a warning. Her name was Mrs. Sinico. Her husband's great-great-grandfather had come from Leghorn. Her husband was captain of a mercantile boat plying between Dublin and Holland; and they had one child.

Meeting her a third time by accident he found courage to make an appointment. She came. This was the first of many meetings; they met always in the evening and chose the most quiet quarters for their walks together. Mr. Duffy, however, had a distaste for underhand ways and, finding that they were compelled to meet stealthily, he forced her to ask him to her house. Captain Sinico encouraged his visits, thinking that his daughter's hand was in question. He had dismissed his wife so sincerely from his gallery of pleasures that he did not suspect that anyone else would take an interest in her. As the husband was often away and the daughter out giving music lessons Mr. Duffy had many opportunities of enjoying the lady's society. Neither he nor she had had any such adventure before and neither was conscious of any incongruity. Little by little he entangled his thoughts with hers. He lent her books, provided her with ideas, shared his intellectual life with her. She listened to all.

Sometimes in return for his theories she gave out some fact of her own life. With almost maternal solicitude she urged him to let his nature open to the full: she became his confessor. He told her that for some time he had assisted at the meetings of an Irish Socialist Party where he had felt himself a unique figure amidst a score of sober workmen in a garret lit by an inefficient oil-lamp. When the party had divided into three sections, each under its own leader and in its own garret, he had discontinued his attendances. The workmen's discussions, he said, were too timorous; the interest they took in the question of wages was inordinate. He felt that they were hard-featured realists and that they resented an exactitude which was the produce of a leisure not within their reach. No social revolution, he told her, would be likely to strike Dublin for some centuries.

She asked him why did he not write out his thoughts. For what, he asked her, with careful scorn. To compete with phrasemongers, incapable of thinking consecutively for sixty seconds? To submit himself to the criticisms of an obtuse middle class which entrusted its morality to policemen and its fine arts to impresarios?

He went often to her little cottage outside Dublin; often they spent their evenings alone. Little by little, as their thoughts entangled, they spoke of subjects less remote. Her companionship was like a warm soil about an exotic. Many times she allowed the dark to fall upon them, refraining from lighting the lamp. The dark discreet room, their isolation, the music that still vibrated in their ears united them. This union exalted him, wore away the rough edges of his character, emotionalised his mental life. Sometimes he caught himself listening to the sound of his own voice. He thought that in her eyes he would ascend to an angelical stature; and, as he attached the fervent nature of his companion more and more closely to him, he heard the strange impersonal voice which he recognised as his own, insisting on the soul's incurable loneliness. We cannot give ourselves, it said: we are our own. The end of these discourses was that one night during which she had shown every sign of unusual excitement, Mrs. Sinico caught up his hand passionately and pressed it to her cheek.

Mr. Duffy was very much surprised. Her interpretation of his words disillusioned him. He did not visit her for a week; then he wrote to her asking her to meet him. As he did not wish their last interview to be troubled by the influence of their ruined confessional they met in a little cakeshop near the Parkgate. It was cold autumn weather but in spite of the cold they wandered up and down the roads of the Park for nearly three hours. They agreed to break off their intercourse: every bond, he said, is a bond to sorrow. When they came out of the Park they walked in silence towards the tram; but here she began to tremble so violently that, fearing another collapse on her part, he bade her good-bye quickly and left her. A few days later he received a parcel containing his books and music.

Four years passed. Mr. Duffy returned to his even way of life. His room still bore witness of the orderliness of his mind. Some new pieces of music encumbered the music-stand in the lower room and on his shelves stood two volumes by Nietzsche: *Thus Spake Zarathustra* and *The Gay Science*. He wrote seldom in the sheaf of papers which lay in his desk. One of his sentences, written two months after his last interview with Mrs. Sinico, read: Love between man and man is impossible because there must not be sexual intercourse and friendship between man and woman is impossible because there must be sexual intercourse. He kept away from concerts lest he should meet her. His father died; the junior partner of the bank retired. And still every morning he went into the city by tram and every evening walked home from the city after having dined moderately in George's Street and read the evening paper for dessert.

One evening as he was about to put a morsel of corned beef and cabbage into his mouth his hand stopped. His eyes fixed themselves on a paragraph in the evening paper which he had propped against the water-carafe. He replaced the morsel of food on his plate and read the paragraph attentively. Then he drank a glass of water, pushed his plate to one side, doubled the paper down before him between his elbows and read the paragraph over and over again. The cabbage began to deposit a cold white grease on his plate. The girl came over to him to ask was his dinner not properly cooked. He said it was very good and ate a few mouthfuls of it with difficulty. Then he paid his bill and went out.

He walked along quickly through the November twilight, his stout hazel stick striking the ground regularly, the fringe of

SIMON VAN BOOY

the buff *Mail* peeping out of a side-pocket of his tight reefer over-coat. On the lonely road which leads from the Parkgate to Chapelizod he slackened his pace. His stick struck the ground less emphatically and his breath, issuing irregularly, almost with a sighing sound, condensed in the wintry air. When he reached his house he went up at once to his bedroom and, taking the paper from his pocket, read the paragraph again by the failing light of the window. He read it not aloud, but moving his lips as a priest does when he reads the prayers *Secreto*. This was the paragraph:

DEATH OF A LADY AT SYDNEY PARADE
A Painful Case

To-day at the City of Dublin Hospital the Deputy Coroner (in the absence of Mr. Leverett) held an inquest on the body of Mrs. Emily Sinico, aged forty-three years, who was killed at Sydney Parade Station yesterday evening. The evidence showed that the deceased lady, while attempting to cross the line, was knocked down by the engine of the ten o'clock slow train from Kingstown, thereby sustaining injuries of the head and right side which led to her death.

James Lennon, driver of the engine, stated that he had been in the employment of the railway company for fifteen years.

On hearing the guard's whistle he set the train in motion and a second or two afterwards brought it to rest in response to loud cries. The train was going slowly.

P. Dunne, railway porter, stated that as the train was about to start he observed a woman attempting to cross the lines. He ran towards her and shouted, but, before he could reach her, she was caught by the buffer of the engine and fell to the ground.

A juror. "You saw the lady fall?"

Witness. "Yes."

Police Sergeant Croly deposed that when he arrived he found the deceased lying on the platform apparently dead. He had the body taken to the waiting-room pending the arrival of the ambulance.

Constable 57E corroborated.

Dr. Halpin, assistant house surgeon of the City of Dublin Hospital, stated that the deceased had two lower ribs fractured and had sustained severe contusions of the right shoulder. The right side of the head had been injured in the fall. The injuries were not sufficient to have caused death in a normal person. Death, in his opinion, had been probably due to shock and sudden failure of the heart's action.

Mr. H. B. Patterson Finlay, on behalf of the railway company, expressed his deep regret at the accident. The company had always taken every precaution to prevent people crossing the lines except by the bridges, both by placing notices in every station and by the use of patent spring gates at level crossings. The deceased had been in the habit of crossing the lines late at night from platform to platform and, in view of certain other circumstances of the case, he did not think the railway officials were to blame.

Captain Sinico, of Leoville, Sydney Parade, husband of the deceased, also gave evidence. He stated that the deceased was his wife. He was not in Dublin at the time of the accident as he had arrived only that morning from Rotterdam. They had been married for twenty-two years and had lived happily until about two years ago when his wife began to be rather intemperate in her habits.

Miss Mary Sinico said that of late her mother had been in the habit of going out at night to buy spirits. She, witness, had often tried to reason with her mother and had induced her to join a League. She was not at home until an hour after the accident.

The jury returned a verdict in accordance with the medical evidence and exonerated Lennon from all blame.

The Deputy Coroner said it was a most painful case, and expressed great sympathy with Captain Sinico and his daughter. He urged on the railway company to take strong measures to prevent the possibility of similar accidents in the future. No blame attached to anyone.

Mr. Duffy raised his eyes from the paper and gazed out of his window on the cheerless evening landscape. The river lay quiet beside the empty distillery and from time to time a light appeared in some house on the Lucan road. What an end! The whole narrative of her death revolted him and it revolted him to think that he had ever spoken to her of what he held sacred. The threadbare phrases, the inane expressions of sympathy, the cautious words of a reporter won over to conceal the details of a commonplace vulgar death attacked his stomach. Not merely had she degraded herself; she had degraded him. He saw the squalid tract of her vice, miserable and malodorous. His soul's companion! He thought of the hobbling wretches whom he had seen carrying cans and bottles to be filled by the barman. Just God, what an end! Evidently she had been unfit to live, without any strength of purpose, an easy prey to habits, one of the wrecks on which civilisation has been reared. But that she could have sunk so low! Was it possible he had deceived himself so utterly about her? He remembered her outburst of that night and interpreted it in a harsher sense than he had ever done. He had no difficulty now in approving of the course he had taken.

As the light failed and his memory began to wander he thought her hand touched his. The shock which had first attacked his stomach was now attacking his nerves. He put on his over-coat and hat quickly and went out. The cold air met him on the threshold; it crept into the sleeves of his coat. When he came to the public-house at Chapelizod Bridge he went in and ordered a hot punch.

The proprietor served him obsequiously but did not venture to talk. There were five or six workingmen in the shop discussing the value of a gentleman's estate in County Kildare. They drank at intervals from their huge pint tumblers and smoked, spitting often on the floor and sometimes dragging the sawdust over their spits with their heavy boots. Mr. Duffy sat on his stool and gazed at them, without seeing or hearing them. After a while they went out and he called for another punch. He sat a long time over it. The shop was very quiet. The proprietor sprawled on the counter reading the *Herald* and yawning. Now and again a tram was heard swishing along the lonely road outside.

As he sat there, living over his life with her and evoking alternately the two images in which he now conceived her, he realised that she was dead, that she had ceased to exist, that she had become a memory. He began to feel ill at ease. He asked himself what else could he have done. He could not have carried on a comedy of deception with her; he could not have lived with her openly. He had done what seemed to him best. How was he to blame? Now that she was gone he understood how lonely her life must have been, sitting night after night alone in that room. His life would be lonely too until he, too, died, ceased to exist, became a memory—if anyone remembered him.

It was after nine o'clock when he left the shop. The night was cold and gloomy. He entered the Park by the first gate and walked along under the gaunt trees. He walked through the bleak alleys where they had walked four years before. She seemed to be near him in the darkness. At moments he seemed to feel her voice touch his ear, her hand touch his. He stood still to listen. Why had he withheld life from her? Why had he sentenced her to death? He felt his moral nature falling to pieces.

When he gained the crest of the Magazine Hill he halted and looked along the river towards Dublin, the lights of which burned redly and hospitably in the cold night. He looked down the slope and, at the base, in the shadow of the wall of the Park, he saw some human figures lying. Those venal and furtive loves filled him with despair. He gnawed the rectitude of his life; he felt that he had been outcast from life's feast. One human being had seemed to love him and he had denied her life and happiness: he had sentenced her to ignominy, a death of shame. He knew that the prostrate creatures down by the wall were watching him and wished him gone. No one wanted him; he was outcast from life's feast. He turned his eyes to the grey gleaming river, winding along towards Dublin. Beyond the river he saw a goods train winding out of Kingsbridge Station, like a worm with a fiery head winding through the darkness, obstinately and laboriously. It passed slowly out of sight; but still he heard in his ears the laborious drone of the engine reiterating the syllables of her name.

He turned back the way he had come, the rhythm of the engine pounding in his ears. He began to doubt the reality of what memory told him. He halted under a tree and allowed the rhythm to die away. He could not feel her near him in the darkness nor her voice touch his ear. He waited for some minutes listening. He could hear nothing: the night was perfectly silent. He listened again: perfectly silent. He felt that he was alone.

There came a time when the risk to remain tight in the bud
was more painful than the risk it took to blossom.

—*Anaïs Nin*

Cures all sorrow with more.

—*John Donne*

Love one another, but make not a bond of love.
Let it rather be a moving sea between the shores of your
souls.

—*Kahlil Gibran*

Jiddu Krishnamurti was born in India in 1895. He is considered by many as a divinely inspired being or a guru. For most of his life, Krishnamurti traveled the world, addressing large audiences on the need to transform themselves through self-knowledge, by being aware of the subtleties of their thoughts and feelings in daily life.

In *On Love and Loneliness*, Krishnamurti suggests that *why* we need love may not be as useful as why we *think* we need love. Krishnamurti believes that our minds often get stuck in a pattern of seeing things a certain way, and without investigation, we may find that our mind is a barrier to "authentic" love—because we are too busy seeking what we think is love based on an unexamined view of the world. Krishnamurti argues that a person's need for love, a person's longing for love as a means to an end, is not actually a need for love but a need for stimulation, and that a need for fulfillment through another person is not "love."

Jiddu Krishnamurti

from *On Love and Loneliness*

with students at Rajghat School, December 19, 1952

We were discussing the complex problem of love. I do not think we shall understand it until we understand an equally complex problem, which we call the mind. Have you noticed, when we are very young, how inquisitive we are? We want to know, we see many more things than older people. We observe, if we are at all awake, things that older people do not notice. The mind, when we are young, is much more alert, much more curious and wanting to know. That is why, when we are young, we learn so easily mathematics, geography. As we grow older, our minds become more and more crystallized, more and more heavy, more and more bulky. Have you noticed in older people how prejudiced they are? Their minds are fixed, they are not open, they approach everything from a fixed point of view. You are young now; but if you are not very watchful, you will also become like that.

Is it not then very important to understand the mind, and to see whether you cannot be supple, be capable of instant adjustments, of extraordinary capacities in every department of life, of deep research and understanding, instead of gradually becoming dull? Should you not know the ways of the mind, so as to understand the way of love? Because it is the mind that destroys love. Clever people, people who are cunning, do not know what love is because their minds are so sharp, because they are so clever, because they are so superficial—which means to be on the surface—and love is not a thing that exists on the surface.

What is the mind? I am not talking about the brain, the physical construction of the brain about which any physiologist will tell you. The brain is something which reacts to various nervous responses. But you are going to find out what the mind is. The mind says, "I think; it is mine; it is yours; I am hurt; I am jealous; I love; I hate; I am an Indian; I am a Moslem; I believe in this; I do not believe in that; I know; you do not know; I respect; I despise; I want; I do not want." What is this thing? Until you understand it—until you are familiar with the whole process of thinking, which is the mind—until you are aware of that, you will gradually, as you grow older, become hard, crystallized, dull, fixed in a certain pattern of thinking.

What is this thing that you call the mind? It is the way of thinking, the way you think. I am talking of your mind—not somebody else's mind and the way it would think—the way you feel, the way you look at trees, at a fish, at the fishermen, the way you consider the villager. That mind gradually becomes warped or fixed in a certain pattern. When you want something, when you desire, when you crave, when you want to be something, then you set a pattern; that is, your mind

SIMON VAN BOOY

creates a pattern and gets caught. Your desire crystallizes your mind. Say, for example, I want to be a very rich man. The desire of wanting to be a wealthy man creates a pattern and my thinking then gets caught in it, and I can only think in those terms, and I cannot go beyond it. So the mind gets caught in it, gets crystallized in it, gets hard, dull. Or if I believe in something—in God, in a certain political system—the very belief begins to set the pattern, because that belief is the outcome of my desire and that desire strengthens the walls of the pattern. Gradually, my mind becomes dull, incapable of adjustment, of quickness, of sharpness, of clarity, because I am caught in the labyrinth of my own desires.

So until I really investigate this process of my mind, the ways I think, the ways I regard love, until I am familiar with my own ways of thinking, I cannot possibly find what love is. There will be no love when my mind desires certain facts of love, certain actions of it, and when I then imagine what love should be. Then I give certain motives to love. So, gradually, I create the pattern of action with regard to love. But it is not love; it is merely my desire of what love should be. Say, for example, I possess you as a wife or as a husband. Do you understand *possess?* You possess your sari or your coat. If somebody took them away, you would be angry, you would be anxious, you would be irritated. Why? Because you regard your sari or your coat as yours, your property; you possess it; because through possession you feel enriched. Through having many saris, many coats, you feel rich, not only physically rich but inwardly rich. So when somebody takes your coat away, you feel irritated because inwardly you are being deprived of that feeling of being rich, that feeling of possession. Owning creates a barrier, does it not, with regard to love? If I own you, possess you, is that love? I possess you as I possess a car, a coat, a sari, because in possessing, I feel very rich; I depend on it; it is very important to me inwardly. This owning, this possessing, this depending, is what we call love. But if you examine it, you will see that, behind it, the mind feels satisfied in possession. After all, when you possess a sari or many saris or a car or a house, inwardly it gives you a certain satisfaction, the feeling that it is yours.

So the mind desiring, wanting, creates a pattern, and in that pattern it gets caught, and so the mind grows weary, dull, stupid, thoughtless. The mind is the centre of that feeling of the "mine", the feeling that I own something, that I am a big man, that I am a little man, that I am insulted, that I am flattered, that I am clever or that I am very beautiful or that I want to be ambitious or that I am the daughter of somebody or the son of somebody. That feeling of the "me," the "I," is the centre of the mind, is the mind itself. So the more the mind feels "This is mine," and builds walls around that feeling that "I am somebody," that "I must be great," that "I am

SIMON VAN BOOY

a very clever man," or that "I am very stupid or a dull man," the more it creates a pattern, the more and more it becomes enclosed, dull. Then it suffers; then there is pain in that enclosure. Then it says, "What am I to do?" Then it struggles to find something else instead of removing the walls that are enclosing it—by thought, by careful awareness, by going into it, by understanding it. It wants to take something from outside and then to close itself again. So gradually, the mind becomes a barrier to love. So without the understanding of life, of what the mind is, of the way of thinking, of the way from which there is action, we cannot possibly find what love is.

Is not the mind also an instrument of comparison? You say this is better than that; you compare yourself with somebody who is more beautiful, who is more clever. There is comparison when you say, "I remember that particular river that I saw a year ago, and it was still more beautiful." You compare yourself with somebody, compare yourself with an example, with the ultimate ideal. Comparative judgment makes the mind dull; it does not sharpen the mind, it does not make the mind comprehensive, inclusive, because, when you are all the time comparing, what has happened? You see the sunset, and you immediately compare that sunset with the previous sunset. You see a mountain and you see how beautiful it is. Then you say, "I saw a still more beautiful mountain two years ago." When you are comparing, you are really not looking at the sunset which is there, but you are looking at it in order to compare it with something else. So comparison prevents you from looking fully. I look at you, you are nice, but I say, "I know a much nicer person, a much better person, a more noble person, a more stupid person." When I do this, I am not looking at you. Because my mind is occupied with something else, I am not looking at you at all. In the same way, I am not looking at the sunset at all. To really look at the sunset, there must be no comparison; to really look at you, I must not compare you with someone else. It is only when I look at you without comparative judgment that I can understand you. But when I compare you with somebody else, then I judge you and I say, "Oh, he is a very stupid man." So stupidity arises when there is comparison. I compare you with somebody else, and that very comparison brings about a lack of human dignity. When I look at you without comparing, I am only concerned with you, not with someone else. The very concern about you, not comparatively, brings about human dignity.

So as long as the mind is comparing, there is no love, and the mind is always judging, comparing, weighing, looking to find out where the weakness is. So where there is comparison, there is no love. When the mother and father love their children, they do not compare them, they do not compare their child with another child; it is their child and they love their

SIMON VAN BOOY

child. But you want to compare yourself with something better, with something nobler, with something richer, so you create in yourself a lack of love. You are always concerned with yourself in relationship to somebody else. As the mind becomes more and more comparative, more and more possessive, more and more depending, it creates a pattern in which it gets caught, so it cannot look at anything anew, afresh. And so it destroys that very thing, that very perfume of life, which is love.

Student: Is there not an end of love? Is love based on attraction?

Krishnamurti: Suppose you are attracted by a beautiful river, by a beautiful woman, or by a man. What is wrong with that? We are trying to find out. You see, when I am attracted to a woman, to a man, or to a child or to truth, I want to be with it, I want to possess it, I want to call it my own; I say that it is mine and that it is not yours. I am attracted to that person, I must be near that person, my body must be near that person's body. So what have I done? What generally happens? The fact is that I am attracted and I want to be near that person; that is a fact, not an ideal. And it is also a fact that when I am attracted and I want to possess, there is no love. My concern is with the fact and not with what I should be. When I possess a person, I do not want that person to look at anybody else.

When I consider that person as mine, is there love? Obviously not. The moment my mind creates a hedge round that person, as "mine," there is no love.

The fact is, my mind is doing that all the time. That is what we are discussing, to see how the mind is working; and perhaps, being aware of it, the mind itself will be quiet.

S: Why does one feel the necessity of love?

K: You mean, why do we have to have love? Why should there be love? Can we do without it? What would happen if you did not have this so-called love? If your parents began to think out why they love you, you might not be here. They might throw you out. They think they love you; therefore they want to protect you, they want to see you educated, they feel that they must give you every opportunity to be something. This feeling of protection, this feeling of wanting you to be educated, this feeling that you belong to them, is what they generally call love. Without it, what would happen? What would happen if your parents did not love you? You would be neglected, you would be something inconvenient, you would be pushed out, they would hate you. So, fortunately, there is this feeling of love, perhaps clouded, perhaps besmirched and ugly, but there is still that feeling, fortunately for you and me; otherwise you and I would not have been educated, would not exist.

SIMON VAN BOOY

S: I am not loved and I want to be, for without it life has no meaning. How can I fulfil this longing?

K: I hope you are not merely listening to words, because then they will be another distraction, a waste of time. But if you are really experiencing the things that we are discussing, then they will have an extraordinary significance; because though you may follow words with the conscious mind, if you are experiencing what is being said, the unconscious also takes part in it. Given an opportunity, the unconscious will reveal its whole content, and so bring about a complete understanding of ourselves. So I hope you are not merely listening to a talk, but are actually experiencing the things as we go along.

The questioner wants to know how to love and to be loved. Is not that the state of most of us? We all want to be loved, and also to give love. We talk a great deal about it. All religions, all preachers, talk about it. So let us find out what we mean by love.

Is love sensation? Is love a thing of the mind? Can you think about love? You can think about the object of love, but you cannot think about love, can you? I can think about the person I love; I can have a picture, an image of that person, and recall the sensations, the memories, of our relationship. But is love sensation, memory? When I say, "I want to love and be loved," is that not merely thought, a reflection of the mind? Is thought love? We think it is, do we not? To us, love is sensation. That is why we have pictures of the people whom we love, that is why we think about them and are attached to them. That is all a process of thought, is it not?

Now, thought is frustrated in different directions, and therefore it says, "I find happiness in love, so I must have love." That is why we cling to the person we love; that is why we possess the person, psychologically as well as physiologically. We create laws to protect the possession of what we love, whether it be a person, a piano, a piece of property, or an idea, a belief, because in possession—with all its complications of jealousy, fear, suspicion, anxiety—we feel secure. So we have made love into a thing of the mind, and with the things of the mind we fill the heart. Because the heart is empty, the mind says, "I must have that love," and we try to fulfil ourselves through the wife, through the husband. Through love we try to become something. That is, love becomes a useful thing; we use love as a means to an end.

So we have made of love a thing of the mind. The mind becomes the instrument of love, and the mind is only sensation. Thought is the reaction of memory to sensation. Without the symbol, the word, the image, there is no memory, there is no thought. We know the sensation of so-called love, and we cling to that, and when it fails we want some other expression of that same sensation. So the more we cultivate sensation, the more we cultivate so-called knowledge—which is merely memory—the less there is of love.

As long as we are seeking love, there must be a self-enclosing process. Love implies vulnerability, love implies communion, and there can be no communion, no vulnerability, as long as there is the self-enclosing process of thought. The very process of thought is fear, and how can there be communion with another when there is fear, when we use thought as a means for further stimulation?

There can be love only when you understand the whole process of the mind. Love is not of the mind, and you cannot think about love. When you say, "I want love," you are thinking about it, you are longing for it, which is a sensation, a means to an end. Therefore it is not love that you want, but stimulation; you want a means through which you can fulfil yourself, whether it be a person, a job, or a particular excitement, and so on. Surely, that is not love. Love can be only when the thought of the self is absent, and freedom from the self lies through self-knowledge. With self-knowledge there comes understanding, and when the total process of the mind is completely and fully revealed and understood, then you will know what it is to love. Then you will see that love has nothing to do with sensation, that it is not a means of fulfilment. Then love is by itself, without any result. Love is a state of being, and in that state, the "me," with its identifications, anxieties, and possessions, is absent. Love cannot be, as long as the activities of the self, of the "me," whether conscious or unconscious, continue to exist. That is why it is important to understand the process of the self, the centre of recognition which is the "me."

English Baroque composer Henry Purcell was born around 1659 in London. When Purcell was six, his father died, and he was placed in the care of a kind uncle who was also a musician like Purcell's father. Until his early death in 1695, Purcell composed many works and had a very successful career.

Purcell's opera *Dido and Aeneas* was first performed at a girls' school in 1689. The opera is based on the fourth book of Virgil's *Aeneid*, and celebrates the tragic story of Dido, who falls desperately in love after Aeneas is shipwrecked in her country. When Aeneas eventually leaves, Dido cannot live without him and awaits her death, uttering one of the most famous lines in all of operatic music. *Dido and Aeneas* is considered a monumental work of English Baroque opera.

Dido's repetition of this line draws the audience closer with each mesmerizing utterance until her final words feel as though they are being whispered to each listener in a moment of intimate confession, as she lies suspended between this world and the next.

Henry Purcell

from *Dido and Aeneas*

Remember me, but ah! forget my fate.

—Dido

William Butler Yeats was an Irish poet and playwright born in 1865. He was interested not only in poetry, but also in the politics of Ireland and the occult. Yeats's work is revered for its symbolism, for its use of the mythology of Irish folklore, and for its sensuality. He was awarded the Nobel Prize for Literature in 1923. He died in 1939.

William Butler Yeats

"When You Are Old"

When you are old and grey and full of sleep,
And nodding by the fire, take down this book,
And slowly read, and dream of the soft look
Your eyes had once, and of their shadows deep;

How many loved your moments of glad grace,
And loved your beauty with love false or true,
But one man loved the pilgrim soul in you,
And loved the sorrows of your changing face;

And bending down beside the glowing bars,
Murmur, a little sadly, how Love fled
And paced upon the mountains overhead
And hid his face amid a crowd of stars.

ACKNOWLEDGMENTS

Amy Baker; Joshua Bodwell; Dr. and Mrs. J. E. Booy; Dr. and Mrs. Raha Booy; Theodore Bouloukos; Douglas and Anita Borroughs, esq.; Milan Bozic; Ken Browar; Bobby Brinson; David Bruson; Dr. S. A. Burgess, academic director and professor at Mediterranean Center for Arts and Sciences; Gabriel Byrne; Tricia Callahan; Michael Colford; Boston Public Library; Christine Corday; Ken and Joann Davis; Justin Dodd; Writing Program at University College Falmouth; Patricio Ferrari; Peggy Flaum; Dr. Giovanni Frazzetto; Colin Gee; Kayleigh George; East Hampton Library; Werner Herzog; Jen Hart; Gregory Henry; Lucas Hunt; Dr. Mickey Kempner; Alan Kleinberg; Hilary Knight; Bryan LeBoeuf; Eva

Lontscharitsch; Alain Malraux; Lisa Mamo; Metropolitan Museum of Art; Metropolitan Opera; MoMA; Dr. Edmund Miller; Cal Morgan; National Gallery, London: Dr. William Neal; New York Society Library; New York School of Visual Arts; Lukas Ortiz; Rogers Memorial Library of Southampton; Jonathan Rabinowitz; Alberto Rojas; Ivan Shaw; Hala Schlub; Philip G. Spitzer; Virginia Stanley; Dolores Henry; the Connolly family; the Gaddis family; the O'Brien Family; McNally-Jackson Booksellers; Prairie Lights Books; Shakespeare & Co. Paris; Andy Spade; Anthony Sperdutti; Fred Volkmer; Amy Vreeland; Wim Wenders; Dr. Barbara Wersba; Phaedra Athanasiou at the Brooklyn Academy of Music; and Les Arts Florissants, under the musical direction of William Christie.

I would like to express an even greater debt of gratitude to the following two people:

Carrie Kania, for her brilliance, her vision, her love of Samuel Beckett and Henry Miller, and her unrivaled sense of personal style and her collection of Vivienne Westwood shoes.

My deepest thanks go to Michael Signorelli for his sparkling intelligence, superhuman attention to detail, old-world courtesy, and the fact that he's a fly-fisherman.

ACKNOWLEDGMENTS

PERMISSIONS

Every effort has been made to trace the ownership of copyrighted material and to make full acknowledgment of its use. The editor regrets any errors or omissions, which will be corrected in subsequent editions upon notification in writing to the publisher.

"The Kind Elephant," from *Twenty Jataka Tales* by Noor Inayat Khan. © Noor Inayat Khan. Reprinted by permission of Inner Traditions Bear & Company.

"Throw Me on a Scale" and "Two Giant Fat People," from *The Gift: Poems by Hafiz*. Published by the Pen-

Why?

Each volume consists of famous excerpts and passages from philosophical, biblical, and literary sources with an introduction and commentary by Simon van Booy.

Visit www.AuthorTracker.com for exclusive information on your favorite HarperCollins authors.

Available wherever books are sold, or call 1-800-331-3761 to order.

Why We Need Love
ISBN: 978-0-06-184554-3
(paperback)

Why We Fight
ISBN: 978-0-06-184556-7
(paperback)

**Why Our Decisions
Don't Matter**
ISBN: 978-0-06-184555-0
(paperback)